To my wife Doris E. Fleischman

Some of the ideas and some of the material in this book have been used in articles written for *The Bookman, The Delineator, Advertising and Selling, The Independent, The American Journal of Sociology,* and other journals, to whom the author makes grateful acknowledgment.

CONTENTS

INTRODUCTION

I.

Prior to World War One, the word *propaganda* was little-used in English, except by certain social activists, and close observers of the Vatican; and, back then, *propaganda* tended not to be the damning term we throw around today. The word had been coined in 1622, when Pope Gregory XV, frightened by the global spread of Protestantism, urgently proposed an addition to the Roman curia. The Office for the Propagation of the Faith (*Congregatio de propaganda fide*) would supervise the Church's missionary efforts in the New World and elsewhere: "They are to take account of and to deal with each and every concern for the spread of the faith throughout the world." Far from denoting lies, half-truths, selective history or any of the other tricks that we associate with "propaganda" now, that word meant, at first, the total opposite of such deceptions. Of "the sheep now wretchedly straying" the world over, Gregory wrote:

> Especially it is to be desired that, inspired by divine grace, they should cease to wander amidst heresies through the unhappy pastures of infidelity, drinking deadly and poisonous water, but be placed in the pasture of the true faith, that they may be gathered together in saving doctrine, and be led to the springs of the waters of life.[i]

The word seems to have retained its strongly Catholic aura well into the nineteenth century; and, often, when the user stressed that Roman origin, the word would be pejorative. "Derived from this celebrated society [the *Congregatio de propaganda fide*], the name *propaganda* applied in modern political language as a term of reproach to secret associations for the spread of opinions and principles which are viewed by most governments with horror and aversion," writes the British chemist William Thomas Brande in 1842.[ii] However, while the word then *could* be used to make a sinister impression, it did not automatically evoke subversive falsehood, as it has since the 1920s. In his *English Traits* (1856), for instance, Emerson uses *propagandist* as an adjective not at all suggestive of the stealthy spread of some pernicious creed or notion. He describes the British as "still aggressive and propagandist, enlarging the dominion of their arts and liberty"—a passage that associates propaganda not with alien subversion but the most enlightened rule:

> Their laws are hospitable, and slavery does not exist under them. What oppression exists is incidental and temporary; their success is not sudden or fortunate, but they have maintained constancy and self-equality for many ages.[iii]

Prior to the war, the word's derogatory use was far less common than its neutral denotation. Here, for example, is the calm (and accurate) definition given in the *Oxford English Dictionary*: "Any association, systematic scheme, or concerted movement for the propagation of a particular doctrine or practice." Thus was *propaganda* generally perceived not as an instrument for striking "horror and aversion" in the souls of government officials, but as an enterprise whose consequences might seem horrid—or innocuous, or even beneficial, depending on its authors and their aim (and the perceiver's point of view). A campaign to improve public health through vaccination, sanitary cooking or the placement of spittoons was, or is, no less a propaganda drive than any anti-clerical or socialist or nativist crusade. Evidently this fact was apparent to those few who used the word—which did not become a synonym for big black lies until the Allies made the word familiar to the masses of Great Britain and America. Until then, *propaganda* was a term so unimportant that there is no definition for it in the great 1911 *Encyclopedia Britannica* (which does include a short entry for *propagate*).

The war had a complex effect on the repute of propaganda. Although the practice had, albeit unnamed, been variously used by governments for centuries (Napoleon was especially incisive on the subject, as well as an inspired practitioner), it was not until 1915 that governments first systematically deployed the entire range of modern media to rouse their populations to fanatical assent. Here was an extraordinary state accomplishment: mass enthusiasm at the prospect of a global brawl that otherwise would mystify those very masses, and that shattered most of those who actually took part in it. The Anglo-American drive to demonize "the Hun," and to cast the war as a transcendent clash between Atlantic "civilization" and Prussian "barbarism," made so powerful an impression on so many that the worlds of government and business were forever changed.

Now "public opinion" stood out as a force that must be managed, and not through clever guesswork but by experts trained to do that all-important job. Thus the war improved the status of those working in the fields of public suasion. Formerly, the lords of industry and commerce had often seen the advertising agent as a charlatan, associated with the tawdry bunkum used to peddle patent medicines and cigarettes, and trying to sell a service that any boss with half a brain could surely manage on his own. The nascent field of public relations also had been disesteemed by those atop the social pyramid, who saw that sort of work as necessary only on the vaudeville circuit and on Broadway. The great Allied campaign to celebrate (or sell) Democracy, etc., was a venture so successful, and, it seemed, so noble, that it suddenly legitimized such propagandists, who, once the war had ended, went right to work massaging or exciting various publics on behalf of entities like General Motors, Procter & Gamble, John D. Rockefeller, General Electric.

And so, from the signing of the Versailles Treaty to the Crash of 1929, there was high excitement in the booming field of peace-time propaganda. That reborn generation of admen and publicists, no longer common hucksters but *professionals*, sold their talents to Big Business through a long barrage of books, essays, speeches and events extolling the miraculous effects of advertising and/or publicity—i.e., propaganda, as the proponents of the craft, and their corporate clients, often kept referring to it, quietly. According to the propagandists' evangelical selfsalesmanship (many of them were in fact the sons of ministers), their revolutionary "science" would do far more than make some people richer. Just as during the war, propaganda would at once exalt the nation and advance the civilizing process, teaching immigrants and other folks of modest means how to transform themselves, through smart consumption, into happy and presentable Americans. Throughout the Twenties, as propaganda's earnest advocates devoutly pushed that *faux*-progressive line, "propaganda" seemed—at least to those who peddled it—a wondrous new progressive force, capable of brightening every life and every home. That quasi-religious pitch was memorably made in books like Earnest Elmo Calkins's *Business the Civilizer* (1928), Bruce Barton's best-selling parable *The Man Nobody Knows* (1925), and, less distinctively, in countless other works of what we might call propaganda propaganda. Like its wartime prototype, the post-war propaganda drive was an immense success, as it persuaded not just businessmen but journalists and politicians that "the manufacture of consent," in Walter Lippmann's famous phrase, was a necessity throughout the public sphere.[iv]

And yet, for all its honking boosterism, that sales campaign was oddly hobbled from the start, because the product's very name had come into the news, and into common conversation, as a dirty word.[v] Ironically, the same great war drive that had made that alien term "propaganda" commonplace had also made the neutral term pejorative. At the very moment of the propagandists' triumph as professionals, in other words, to be referred to as a "propagandist" was an insult. This was no accident, but a paradoxical result of the war propagandists' winning enterprise: for the propagandists had themselves besmirched the word by using it always and only in dark reference to *the enemy*. "We did not call it propaganda, for that word, in German hands, had come to be associated with deceit and corruption," writes George Creel, director of the U.S. Office of War Information, in *How We Advertised America* (1920). The *Germans* having trashed the word, Creel claims, the *Americans* never used it to refer to their own output, but—rightly—favored other, more exalted terms instead: "Our effort was educational and informative throughout, for we had such confidence in our case as to feel that no other argument was needed than the simple, straightforward presentation of facts."[vi]

That passage is itself, of course, a stunning bit of propaganda, as it bluntly reconfirms the Manichaean plot that Creel & Co. had hammered home throughout the war: Germans always lie, Americans always tell the truth. *How* the German propaganda "had come to be associated with deceit and corruption" is a question Creel would rather not address, preferring instead to bury it in that sly (if sly it was) passive construction. There is much to say about Creel's obfuscation, or evasion, of the fact that *his own propagandists* had "associated" German propaganda with "corruption" and "deceit"—and did so just as Creel does in that passage. At this point, however, our main concern is not propaganda's crucial self-effacement, but the darkening effect of Allied propaganda on the elusive word itself.

In World War One it was the propaganda of *our side* that first made "propaganda" so opprobrious a term. Fouled by close association with "the Hun," the word did not regain its innocence—not even when the Allied propaganda used to tar "the Hun" had been belatedly exposed to the

American and British people. Indeed, as they learned more and more about the outright lies, exaggerations and half-truths used on them by their own governments, both populations came, understandably, to see "propaganda" as a weapon even *more* perfidious than they had thought when they had not perceived themselves as its real target. Thus did the word's demonic implications only harden through the Twenties, in spite of certain random efforts to redeem it.

II.

Edward Bernays's *Propaganda* (1928) was the most ambitious of such efforts. Through meticulous descriptions of a broad variety of post-war propaganda drives—all of them ingenious, apparently benign in purpose and honest in their execution—Bernays attempts to rid the word of its bad smell. His motivation would appear to be twofold. Bernays always deemed himself to be both "a truth-seeker and a propagandist for propaganda," as he put it in another apologia in 1929.[vii] On the one hand, then, his interest would be purely scientific; and so his effort to redeem the word is based to some extent on intellectual necessity, there being no adequate substitute for *propaganda*. In this Bernays was right (and never quite gave up his preference for that word over all the euphemisms).[viii] His wish to reclaim the appropriate term bespeaks a serious commitment to precision; Bernays was not one to hype anything—not his clients' wares, and not his craft.

In *Propaganda*, as in all his writings, there is none of the utopian grandiosity that marks so many of the decade's other pro-commercial homilies. Bernays's tone is managerial, not millenarian, nor does he promise that his methodology will turn this world into a modern paradise. His vision seems quite modest. The world informed by "public relations" will be but "a smoothly functioning society," where all of us are guided imperceptibly throughout our lives by a benign elite of rational manipulators.

Bernays derived this vision from the writings of his intellectual hero, Walter Lippmann, whose classic *Public Opinion* had appeared in 1922. From his observations on the Allied propaganda drives' immense success (and his own stint as a U.S. war propagandist), and from his readings of Gustave LeBon, Graham Wallas and John Dewey, among others, Lippmann had arrived at the bleak view that "the democratic El Dorado" is impossible in modern mass society, whose members—by and large incapable of lucid thought or clear perception, driven by herd instincts and mere prejudice, and frequently disoriented by external stimuli—were not equipped to make decisions or engage in rational discourse. "Democracy" therefore requires a supra-governmental body of detached professionals to sift the data, think things through, and keep the national enterprise from blowing up or crashing to a halt. Although mankind surely can be taught to think, that educative process will be long and slow. In the meantime, the major issues must be framed, the crucial choices made, by "the responsible administrator." "It is on the men inside, working under conditions that are sound, that the daily administration of society must rest."[ix]

While Lippmann's argument is freighted with complexities and tinged with the melancholy of a disillusioned socialist, Bernays's adaptation of it is both simple and enthusiastic: "We are governed, our minds are molded, our tastes formed, our ideas suggested, largely by men we have never heard of." These "invisible governors" are a heroic elite, who coolly keep it all together, thereby "organizing chaos," as God did in the Beginning. "It is they who pull the wires which control the public mind, who harness old social forces and contrive new ways to bind and guide the world." While Lippmann is meticulous—indeed, at times near-Proustian—in demonstrating how and why most people have such trouble thinking straight, Bernays takes all that for granted as "a fact." It is a sort of managerial aristocracy that quietly determines what we buy and how we vote and what we deem as good or bad. "They govern us," the author writes, "by their qualities of natural leadership, their ability to supply needed ideas and by their key position in the social structure."

Although purporting vaguely to be one of "us," it soon becomes quite clear that Bernays sees *himself* as an exemplar of that elevated supervisory network, just as he sees his own profession as the most important one up there. Thus Bernays proceeds as both "a truth-seeker and a propagandist for propaganda"; for while he did believe wholeheartedly in his hierarchical conception of "democracy" (and so went on believing through the many further decades of his life, as Stewart Ewen tells us),[x] *Propaganda* is primarily a sales pitch, not an exercise in social theory. In other words, while *Propaganda* is by no means an exhaustive treatment of its subject, the book is edifying for its *own* propaganda tactics, and for the light it sheds obliquely on the hidden zeal with which most winning propagandists do their work, however "scientific" and detached they may appear to be (even to themselves).

Apparently a cool defense of propaganda and its salutary influence on mass society, this book is an extended ad for "public relations" as Bernays himself had learned to practice it with rare intelligence and skill. By 1928, he had become the leading figure in his ever-growing field. Not only had he managed to legitimize his craft ("Counsel on Public Relations" always was his pointed self-description), but his own shop was bustling. His services were therefore not available to everyone; *Propaganda* is aimed mainly at Bernays's potential corporate clientele. And yet the author variously masks that plutocratic bias. At the outset, his seductive use of "us" implies that he, like most of us, is just a fuddled propagandee, and not himself the ablest of "invisible governors." In Chapter I, he further mystifies the status of his usual customers by casting "propaganda" as a sort of populist endeavor, and not as an expensive game that is played best by those who have the most to spend on it. Bernays does this by compiling ostentatiously "inclusive" lists of what he represents as common propaganda sources: catalogues, primarily, of modest civic and professional associations and publications (the Arion Singing Society, the *National Nut News*), with few, if any, bluechip outfits mentioned. And perhaps Bernays was also disingenuous in filling out the volume with its late, brief chapters on how propaganda can serve education, social service, "art and science"—little forays into social and/or cultural concern, intended, seemingly, to make the book seem something other than an essay on how business stands to benefit immensely from the author's sort of expertise. All such quasi-democratic touches notwithstanding, *Propaganda* mainly tells us that Bernays's true métier was to help giant players with their various sales and image problems.

At that sort of effort he was in a class all by himself; Ivy Lee was the only other P.R. man of comparable renown, and his accomplishments were nowhere near as many or as dazzling as the ones described in *Propaganda*, not to mention all the others that the author managed after 1928. The book is most instructive when it tells us how and why Bernays did what he did for his (mostly) corporate clients. There are many such revealing moments here—for *every case* of winning propaganda cited in the book was actually Bernays's own handiwork. (The casual reader sees no egotism in such self-promotion, as Bernays discreetly slips into the passive voice each time he tells us what "was done" or "shown" or "proven" with extraordinary deftness.) He had no equal as a propaganda *strategist*. Always thinking far ahead, his aim was not to urge the buyer to demand the product now, but to transform the buyer's very world, so that the product must appear to be desirable as if without the prod of salesmanship. What is the prevailing *custom*, and how might *that* be changed to make this thing or that appear to recommend *itself* to people? "The modern propagandist ... sets to work to create circumstances which will modify that custom." Bernays sold Mozart pianos, for example, not just by hyping the pianos. Rather, he sought carefully "to develop public acceptance of the idea of a music room in the home"—selling the pianos indirectly, through various suggestive trends and enterprises that make it *de rigeur* to have the proper *space* for a piano.

> The music room will be accepted because it has been made the thing. And the man or woman who has a music room, or has arranged a corner of the parlor

as a musical corner, will naturally think of buying a piano. It will come to him as his own idea.

III.

Propaganda, and Bernays himself throughout his long career, sold something more than all the goods and services his clients offered, and also something more than propaganda as a necessary tool for businessmen and politicians. Bernays sold the *myth* of propaganda as a wholly rational endeavor, carried out methodically by careful experts skilled enough to lead "public opinion." Consistently he casts himself as a supreme manipulator, *mastering* the responses of a pliable, receptive population. "Conscious and intelligent manipulation," "invisible governors," "they who pull the wires which control the public mind," "shrewd persons operating behind the scenes," "dictators exercising great power," and, below them, people working "as if actuated by the touch of a button"—these are but a few expressions of the icy scientistic paradigm that evidently drove his propaganda practice, and that colored all his thinking on the subject. The propagandist *rules.* The propagandized do whatever he would have them do, exactly as he tells them to, and without knowing it.

Derived from the positivism of the nineteenth century (and indirectly bolstered by the work of Bernays's uncle, Sigmund Freud), this neo-Baconian conception of the propagandist's power was surely not Bernays's invention. That cool and manly image was a commonplace from the Twenties through the Cold War, as was the obverse image of "the crowd" as *female* in its feverish responsiveness. Why was this tableau of domination so pervasive? For self-conscious "professionals" such as Bernays, expert detachment was, of course, a point of pride—and a strong selling-point, as that hard attitude provided tacit reassurance to potential clients that the propagandist worked not just by instinct or mood, but as impartially, and, if need be, ruthlessly, as any doctor or attorney. He could work others up without getting all worked up himself (or "going native," as, say, officials in the U.S. State empathizing with the foreign populace that he was sent to dupe).

The myth of the detached manipulator and compliant crowd has, since the Twenties, also been abundantly reechoed by academic students of mass suasion. "Convictions in a demagogue are a weakness and may prove a very serious injury," asserted social psychologist Frederick C. Venn in 1928. "They are the last infirmity of some otherwise very splendid demagogues."[xi] So it still is, often, with intellectual studies of successful rabblerousers—the analyst projecting his own rationality onto the firebrand in question, as if assuring *us* that *he* is too intelligent and self-possessed to fall for that spellbinder who excites the vulgar herd. Indeed, the same myth of the unmoved mover has been amply reconfirmed by some of history's most effective agitators: Hitler liked to cast himself as a detached appraiser of his own frenzies at the podium, and Goebbels too believed himself to be completely cold inside, even as his oratory thrilled the crowd. There is no way to confirm this notion that the propagandist is essentially above the fray that he creates. While it surely points us toward some truths about the way that demagogues and other propagandists operate, the notion is unlikely on its face. From what we know about the most ferocious demagogues of yesteryear, successful mass incitement *does* tend to bespeak, and seemingly requires, a fiery core of radical commitment, even if the agitator consciously distorts his facts or trots out this or that rhetorical device. Hitler, Goebbels, Mussolini, Father Coughlin, Joe McCarthy, Gerald L.K. Smith, and many others were *fanatical and cynical at once*, neither wholly in control nor totally ecstatic. Such agitators work within a certain mental borderland, where one can never clearly see conviction as distinct from calculation. Indeed, that inner murkiness appears itself to be the very source or basis of the mass manipulator's enigmatic power, and so we cannot comprehend it through schematic dualistic formulas. (Orwell's elusive concept of "doublethink" is highly pertinent here.)

Of course, there are significant differences between such epoch-making dervishes as Hitler, Coughlin, and McCarthy, who worked in person, on a stage or at a microphone, and propagandists not intent on rousing furious reactions on the spot. Behind even the wildest propaganda orator there must be countless unknown deputies and lesser troops involved in tedious preparations and/or follow-through; and, of course, there are also countless propagandists whose assignments in no way entail the maddening of multitudes. Admakers—researchers, creative directors, copywriters, art directors, photographers— labor gradually toward mass reactions that, in general, are not explosive and immediate but incremental, individual, dispersed, half-conscious. As this book demonstrates, the public relations expert likewise seeks to make a gradual impression, after long research and sober planning. In the hearts of such methodical manipulators there would seem to be no streak of mad commitment, as their enterprise is not infuriating and millennial but businesslike, mundane and rational.

And yet those who do such work are also prone to lose touch with reality; for in their universe the truth is ultimately what the client wants the world to think is true. Whatever cause they serve or goods they sell, effective propagandists must believe in it—or at least momentarily believe that they believe in it. Even he or she who propagates commodities must be to some extent a true believer. "To advertise a product you must believe in it. To convince you must be convinced yourself," observes Marcel Bleustein-Blanchet, longtime head of Publicis, the giant French ad agency.[xii] "I guess I really believe all those schmaltzy things I say in the ads. It seems to have nothing to do with the hardheaded strategies I can work out for marketing products" admits Shirley Polykoff, Clairol's legendary adwoman ("Does she.... Or doesn't she? Only her hairdresser knows for sure!").[xiii]

And even in the magisterial Bernays we note the tendency to let his clients' needs dictate "the truth." Such is the major occupational hazard facing *all* full-time propagandists—even this most cautious and painstaking of professionals, whose celebrated title, "Counsel on Public Relations," implied not just a heightened status but a certain lawyerly impartiality. Bernays invented the authoritative-seeming "sponsoring committee" as a way to hype his client's wares. (He first used this now-venerable gimmick in early 1913, assembling a "committee" of physicians to approve the Broadway production of Eugene Brieux's play *Damaged Goods*, which dealt forthrightly with the issue of venereal disease.) A few years later he used that device again, to sell the American people on the "hearty breakfast" of fried eggs served on strips of bacon. Whereas "the old type of salesmanship" would merely place a lot of ads exhorting everyone to eat more bacon, "because it is good, because it gives you energy," etc., Bernays's approach, as ever, was more "scientific":

> The newer salesmanship, understanding the group structure of society and the principles of mass psychology, would first ask, "Who is it that influences the eating habits of the public?" The answer, obviously, is: "The physicians." The new salesman will then suggest to physicians to say publicly that it is wholesome to eat bacon. He knows as a mathematical certainty, that large numbers of persons will follow the advice of their doctors, because he understands the psychological relation of dependence of men upon their physicians.

This was all very well; and yet the impressive scientism of Bernays's way of *selling* bacon contradicts the inconvenient scientific fact that *eating* bacon has turned out to be not "wholesome" after all, what with its high fat content and cholesterol. Certainly this risk was not yet clear to the American medical establishment when, in the mid-Twenties, Bernays pitched the "hearty breakfast" for the Beechnut Packing Company. It is significant, however, that, in his universe, it is the preeminent consensus that determines what is "true." This is not to fault him for relying on the doctors of his day, nor to suggest that he would have tried to underplay the risks of fatty food if he had known about them. Indeed, Bernays was, in this regard, exceptionally ethical. Once the toxic side effects of smoking had become impossible to talk away, Bernays not only gave up working for tobacco companies, but became a vocal critic of tobacco, lobbying staunchly (and unsuccessfully) to get the Public Relations Society of America to enjoin its members not to work in any way to spread the habit.[xiv]

Bernays can only be applauded for his scrupulous position, which reflected his lifelong commitment to a stringent code of ethics for all p.r. specialists. But the issue here is not so much ethical as epistemological. In a world under the influence of propaganda experts, how does a costly truth get out into the world *as* truth? When is an idea no longer just a crackpot theory, a paranoid delusion of the left or right, but something that must be, and finally is, accepted? Bernays's eventual stand on cigarettes was admirable indeed, especially considering his own prodigious work, from the mid-Thirties, for George Washington Hill's American Tobacco Company. (The propagandist helped Hill sell a lot of Lucky Strikes.) The risks of smoking were, however, evident before the antismoking propaganda started picking up momentum in the Fifties. As early as 1941, the independent journalist George Seldes was intrepidly reporting on the pertinent medical discoveries in his tiny muckraking journal, *In Fact*. With the exception of the *Reader's Digest*, no other American news source, print or broadcast, dared even to hint at what tobacco scientists were finding out—an advertising-induced blackout that persisted, by and large, until the Seventies. Such was the clout of the tobacco companies, which used Bernays's sort of propaganda genius to keep most people blithely unaware of what they were inhaling.

Although Bernays did see the light about tobacco, then, and did the honorable thing, the fact is that corporate propaganda squelches inconvenient journalistic enterprise, so that early warnings fail to resonate, and growing ills receive no mass attention. As with the risks of smoking, so it has been, until very recently, with global warming, and so it is today with the carcinogenicity of cell phones, and the toxic side effects of fluoride, just to name a few underreported threats to public health. In all such cases, the investigative journalist is the propagandist's natural enemy, as the former serves the public interest, while the latter tends to work against it.

Thus Bernays expresses here a hostile view of muckraking journalism, which would always becloud the sunny view that he was hired to propagate. That that view might be false, or incomplete, is a possibility that just does not come up in *Propaganda.* "Big business studies every move which may express its true personality," the author writes, implying clearly that the corporate personality is always somehow likeable, attractive and benign—a notion as unsound as any Ptolemaic theorem or medieval superstition. Concerning cigarettes, the counter-propaganda finally overwhelmed the pro-tobacco propaganda that had long prevented any public talk about the actual effects of smoking. Other of Bernays's campaigns were likewise meant to preempt all discussion, if not all conception, of some rational alternatives to the established ways of doing business.

In 1929, for instance, Bernays mounted "Light's Golden Jubilee." This grand occasion, featuring a muchhyped joint appearance of Thomas Edison and Henry Ford, was ostensibly an earnest and spontaneous celebration of the fiftieth anniversary of Edison's invention of the light bulb. In fact, the "Jubilee" was but a stroke of propaganda on behalf of General Electric and its National Electric Light Association

(NELA), which was the secret means of GE's stranglehold on America's electric power. From 1919 until 1934, NELA carried out the largest peacetime propaganda drive in U.S. history, intended to discourage public ownership of the utilities. That private capital should wield complete control over the nation's power supply was a notion evidently not to be debated.[xv]

Similarly, in 1953 Bernays helped put across the myth that Guatemala was at risk of communist subversion—a serviceable legend that the propagandist actually believed, as he makes clear in his memoirs.[xvi] Bernays was then employed by the United Fruit Company, at whose behest the Eisenhower administration used the CIA to overthrow the democratically elected government of Jacobo Arbenz. Thus was Guatemala forced to start its gruesome modern history as a quasifascist oligarchy. From that point on, the bananas and pineapples would continue to be safely picked by inexpensive native labor under careful watch, with all the profits flowing north. The possibility of some other, less explosive, noncolonial arrangement was clearly not to be imagined by Bernays, just as United Fruit could not imagine it; and so it never could become a public issue here.

IV.

As propaganda for its author's services, *Propaganda* was no doubt successful, adding luster to Bernays's reputation in the business world, and thereby winning him new clients. As propaganda for reclaiming "propaganda," on the other hand, this book did not succeed; nor could any book—or, for that matter, any other sort of propaganda— possibly have made that controversial word uncontroversial again. By 1928, the word's troubling connotations had not faded: on the contrary. Throughout the decade there had been a gradual, disorienting revelation of just how systematically, and how ingeniously, the Allied governments had fooled the peoples of two great democracies, Great Britain and, in particular, the USA. Once the thrill of victory had faded, and the troops came home (if they came home at all) disfigured or disabled, and the reasons for the war were now less clear than they had seemed, the sordid details of the propaganda drive against "the Hun" began to circulate, spread far and wide in a belated flood of memoirs, reminiscences, published diaries, after-dinner speeches and historical accounts.

At first, the Allies' fatal trickery was reported, and deplored, only in such liberal journals as the *New Republic.* By mid-decade, the dispiriting truth about the wartime propaganda was the subject of several highly damning exposés in the *Saturday Evening Post,* a rightist organ widely read. Throughout the press, "propaganda" was now commonly condemned; and, for the most part, *not* as some dark alien force, unloosed upon our virgin culture by the Prussians and/or Reds, but—far worse—*by propagandists of our own.* Now it came to light (and at times the charges were hysterically exaggerated) that various U.S. interests had colluded to mislead the people into a gratuitous slaughter overseas: pro-British economic interests (like the House of Morgan), weapons manufacturers and antileftist groups, as well as all those common hucksters drawn into the service of the government. From the Twenties up until the start of World War II, the word was even more pejorative, as it suggested not just lying, but betrayal.

Thus Bernays's position was eccentric, in the public eye, when this book of his came out in 1928. That same year saw the publication of another, very different book on propaganda: *Falsehood in War-Time*, by the British MP Arthur Ponsonby, is a straightforward catalogue of all the major falsehoods propagated by the Allied governments.[xvii] Ponsonby refutes each lie, explaining also how and why it was devised and spread. That book created quite a furor on its publication in both Britain and America. Bernays's cunning *Propaganda* failed to resonate as strongly as this other, blunter book, which seemed the ultimate summation of the case *against* the craft that Bernays tried, throughout his life, to justify.

The propagandist was no loser at his game, however. True, the word remained simplistically pejorative, and is so used today. Bernays's sanguine view of propaganda, furthermore, and the sophistry he often used to make his arguments, put him on the weak side of debates in public, and earned him much contemptuous abuse from those appalled by the deceitfulness and tawdry aims of corporate propaganda. (There were many more such critics in the Twenties and the Thirties than there are today; and their critiques were publicly accessible—far more than they are today.) Given Bernays's own priorities, however, such treatment was unlikely to have hurt him much. The audience that he most cared about, it seems, was not the public, and surely not those intellectuals who so despised his craft. He wrote for those who understood the value of that craft, and could afford to make it work for them.[xviii] Even as the people, understandably, distrusted "propaganda" more and more, propaganda was becoming ever more pervasive, as its sponsors marveled at its victories.

"In fact," Bernays notes in this book, "its use is growing as its efficiency in gaining public support is recognized." That propaganda easily seduces even those whom it most horrifies is a paradox that Bernays grasped completely; and it is one that we must try at last to understand, if we want to change the world that Edward Bernays, among others, made for us.

Mark Crispin Miller
New York City
July 2004

NOTES

i.
The Latin text of Gregory's bull is included in *Magnum bullarium Romanum: bullarum, privilegiorum ac diplomatum Romanorum Pontificum amplissima collectio* (Graz, Austria: Akademische Drucku. Verlagsanstalt, 1964–1966). It is available online at the Notre Dame Archives, http://classic.archives.nd.edu/bull.htm.

ii.
William Thomas Brande, *A Dictionary of Science, Literature and Art* (London: Longman, Brown, Green, and Longmans, 1842).

iii.
The Collected Works of Ralph Waldo Emerson (Cambridge, Mass.: Harvard University Press, 1994), vol. 5, *English Traits*, p. 25.

iv.
Lippmann refers to "the manufacture of consent" in his *Public Opinion*,which appeared in 1922 (New York: Free Press,1997),p.158).

v.
For an invaluable study of the intellectual uneasiness concerning "propaganda" in the post-war years, see Brett Gary, *The Nervous Liberals: Propaganda Anxieties from World War I to the Cold War* (New York: Columbia University Press, 1999), esp. pp. 15–53.

vi.
George Creel, *How We Advertised America* (New York: Harper & Brothers, 1920), p. 3.

vii.
Bernays, E. L. (1929). "Are We Victims of Propaganda?" *The Forum*, 81 (3), March, 1929, 142–149. Bernays's piece appeared in a robust exchange with social psychologist Everett Dean Martin, who took the anti-propaganda view. This contention is noteworthy, as Martin's *The Behavior of Crowds: A Psychological Study* (1911) had exerted a strong influence on Bernays's thinking. Stuart Ewen, *PR! The Social History of Spin* (New York: Basic Books, 1996), p. 144.

viii.
See Bernays's discussion of the word in his *Biography of an Idea:*

Memoirs of Public Relations Counsel Edward L. Bernays (New York: Simon & Schuster, 1965), pp. 287ff. It is worth noting that, like Creel before him, he ascribes the word's sudden pejorative connotation not to the Allies' own constant claim that "propaganda" was an enemy activity, but to the enemies themselves: "I did not hesitate to call myself a propagandist [in 1918-1919], even though the word had been tarnished by by the German propaganda of the Kaiser and by the Communists."

ix.

Lippmann, *Public Opinion*, p. 251. "The democratic El Dorado" appears on p. 195.

x.

Ewen interviewed the elderly Bernays at length. On the latter's hierarchical world-view, see *PR! The Social History of Spin*, pp. 9–10.

xi.

Frederick E. Venn, "The Demagogue, in W. Brooke Graves, ed., *Readings in Public Opinion: Its Formation and Control* (New York and London: D. Appleton, 1928).

xii.

Marcel Bleustein-Blanchet, *The Rage to Persuade: Memoirs of a Frrench Advertising Man*, trans. Jean Boddewyn (New York and London: Chelsea House, 1982), p. 98.

xiii.

Shirley Polykoff, *Does She.... Or Doesn't She?: And How She Did It* (Garden City, NY: Doubleday, 1975), p. 38.

xiv.

On Bernays's anti-tobacco lobbying efforts, see John Stauber and Sheldon Rampton, *Toxic Sludge Is Good for You: Lies, Damn Lies and the Public Relations Industry* (Monroe, Maine: Common Courage Press, 1995), p. 32.

xv.

And yet it *was* debated, once that mammoth propaganda campaign was exposed by the Federal Trade Commission in a harrowing report of many volumes. Several books were written on the scandal, which has evidently been forgotten. See, for example, Ernest Henry Gruening, *The Public Pays: A Study of Power Propaganda* (New York: The Vanguard

Press, 1931), and Jack Levin, *Power Ethics* (New York: Alfred A Knopf, 1931).

xvi.

Bernays tells the story of his work on Guatemala in *Biography of an Idea*, pp. 744–75. For a clearer and more comprehensive treatment of the coup in Guatemala, and the role played in it by Bernays's client, the United Fruit Company,, see Stephen C. Schlesinger, Stephen Schlesinger and Stephen Kinzer, *Bitter Fruit: The Story of the American Coup in Guatemala*, rev. ed. (Cambridge, Mass.: Harvard University Press, 1999).

xvii.

Arthur Ponsonby, *Falsehood in Wartime: Propaganda Lies of the First World War* (London: George Allen & Unwin, 1928).

xviii.

It is notable that, within the confraternity of propagandists, *propaganda* was a word that *could*, apparently, sometimes be frankly used in its old, neutral sense—even in the Thirties, when U.S. anti-propaganda sentiment was at its height. In one advertising textbook, there is this statement on behalf of "educational pictures" (i.e. propaganda films): "In the field of propagandism there is hardly a more powerful method of arousing and controlling public opinion" (Carl Richard Greer, *Advertising and Its Mechanical Reproduction* [New York: Tudor Publishing, 1931], p. 68). Such casual professional use of the forbidden term is commonplace today within the U.S. intelligence community, notwithstanding the routine pejorative use of "propaganda" *in the propaganda works* deployed by that community.

PROPAGANDA

CHAPTER I

ORGANIZING CHAOS

The conscious and intelligent manipulation of the organized habits and opinions of the masses is an important element in democratic society. Those who manipulate this unseen mechanism of society constitute an invisible government which is the true ruling power of our country.

We are governed, our minds molded, our tastes formed, our ideas suggested, largely by men we have never heard of. This is a logical result of the way in which our democratic society is organized. Vast numbers of human beings must cooperate in this manner if they are to live together as a smoothly functioning society.

Our invisible governors are, in many cases, unaware of the identity of their fellow members in the inner cabinet. They govern us by their qualities of natural leadership, their ability to supply needed ideas and by their key position in the social structure. Whatever attitude one chooses toward this condition, it remains a fact that in almost every act of our daily lives, whether in the sphere of politics or business, in our social conduct or our ethical thinking, we are dominated by the relatively small number of persons—a trifling fraction of our hundred and twenty million—who understand the mental processes and social patterns of the masses. It is they who pull the wires which control the public mind, who harness old social forces and contrive new ways to bind and guide the world.

It is not usually realized how necessary these invisible governors are to the orderly functioning of our group life. In theory, every citizen may vote for whom he pleases. Our Constitution does not envisage political parties as part of the mechanism of government, and its framers seem not to have pictured to themselves the existence in our national politics of anything like the modern political machine. But the American voters soon found that without organization and direction their individual votes, cast, perhaps, for dozens of hundreds of candidates, would produce nothing but confusion. Invisible government, in the shape of rudimentary political parties, arose almost overnight. Ever since then we have agreed, for the sake of simplicity and practicality, that party machines should narrow down the field of choice to two candidates, or at most three or four.

In theory, every citizen makes up his mind on public questions and matters of private conduct. In practice, if all men had to study for themselves the abstruse economic, political, and ethical data involved in every question, they would find it impossible to come to a conclusion without anything. We have voluntarily agreed to let an invisible government sift the data and high-spot the outstanding issue so that our field of choice shall be narrowed to practical proportions. From our leaders and the media they use to reach the public, we accept the evidence and the demarcation of issues bearing upon public question; from some ethical teacher, be it a minister, a favorite essayist, or merely prevailing opinion, we accept a standardized code of social conduct to which we conform most of the time.

In theory, everybody buys the best and cheapest commodities offered him on the market. In practice, if every one went around pricing, and chemically tasting before purchasing, the dozens of soaps or fabrics or brands of bread which are for sale, economic life would be hopelessly jammed. To avoid such confusion, society consents to have its choice narrowed to ideas and objects brought to it's attention through propaganda of all kinds. There is consequently a vast and continuous effort going on to capture our minds in the interest of some policy or commodity or idea.

It might be better to have, instead of propaganda and special pleading, committees of wise men who would choose our rulers, dictate our conduct, private and public, and decide upon the best types of clothes for us to wear and the best kinds of food for us to eat. But we have chosen the opposite method, that of open competition. We must find a way to make free competition function with reasonable smoothness. To achieve this society has consented to permit free competition to be organized by leadership and propaganda.

Some of the phenomena of this process are criticized—the manipulation of news, the inflation of personality, and the general ballyhoo by which politicians and commercial products and social ideas are brought to the consciousness of the masses. The instruments by which public opinion is organized and focused may be misused. But such organization and focusing are necessary to orderly life.

As civilization has become more complex, and as the need for invisible government has been increasingly demonstrated, the technical means have been invented and developed by which opinion may be regimented.

With the printing press and the newspaper, the railroad, the telephone, telegraph, radio and airplanes, ideas can be spread rapidly and even instantaneously all over the whole of America.

H. G. Wells senses the vast potentialities of these inventions when he writes in the *New York Times:*

> "Modern means of communication—the power afforded by print, telephone, wireless and so forth, of rapidly putting through directive strategic or technical conceptions to a great number of cooperating centers, of getting quick replies and effective discussion—have opened up a new world of political processes. Ideas and phrases can now be given an effectiveness greater than the effectiveness of any personality and stronger than any sectional interest. The common design can be documented and sustained against perversion and betrayal. It can be elaborated and developed steadily and widely without personal, local and sectional misunderstanding."

What Mr. Wells says of political processes is equally true of commercial and social processes and all manifestations of mass activity. The groupings and affiliations of society today are no longer subject to "local and sectional" limitations. When the Constitution was adopted, the unit of organization was the village community, which produced the greater part of its own necessary commodities and generated its group ideas and opinions by personal contact and discussion among its citizens. But today, because ideas can be instantaneously transmitted to any distance and to any number of people, this geographical integration has been supplemented by many other kinds of grouping, so that persons having the same ideas and interests may be associated and regimented for common action even though they live thousands of miles apart.

It is extremely difficult to realize how many and diverse are these cleavages in our society. They may be social, political, economical, racial, religious or ethical, with hundreds of subdivisions of each. In the *World Almanac*, for example, the following groups are listed under the A's:

The League to Abolish Capital Punishment; Association to Abolish War; American Institute of Accountants; Actors' Equity Association; Actuarial Association of America; International Advertising Association; National Aeronautic Association; Albany Institute of History and Art; Amen Corner; American Academy in Rome; American Antiquarian Society; League for American Citizenship; American Federation of Labor; Amorc (Rosicrucian Order); Andiron Club; American-Irish Historical Association; Anti-Cigarette League; Anti-Profanity League; Archeological Association of America; National Archery Association; Arion Singing Society; American Astronomical Association; Ayrshire Breeders' Association; Aztec Club of 1847. There are many more under the "A" section of this very limited list.

The *American Newspaper Annual and Directory* for 1928 lists 22,128 periodical publications in America. I have selected at random the N's published in Chicago. They are:

Narod (Bohemian daily newspaper); *Narod-Polski*

(Polish monthly); *N.A.R.D.* (pharmaceutical); *National Corporation Reporter*; *National Culinary Progress* (for hotel chefs); *National Dog Journal*; *National Drug Clerk*; *National Engineer*; *National Grocer*; *National Hotel Reporter*; *National Income Tax Magazine*; *National Jeweler*; *National Journal of Chiropractic*; *National Live Stock Producer*; *National Miller*; *National Nut News*; *National Poultry, Butter and Egg Bulletin*; *National Provisioner* (for meat packers); *National Real Estate Journal*; *National Retail Clothier*; *National Retail Lumber Dealer*; *National Safety News*; *National Spiritualist*; *National Underwriter*; *The Nation's Health*; *Naujienos* (Lithuanian daily newspaper); *New Comer* (Republican weekly for Italians); *Daily News*; *The New World* (Catholic weekly); *North American Banker*; *North American Veterinarian*.

The circulation of some of these publications is astonishing. *The National Live Stock Producer* has a sworn circulation of 155,978; *The National Engineer*, of 20,328; *The New World*, an estimated circulation of 67,000. The greater number of the periodicals listed—chosen at random from among 22,128—have a circulation in excess of 10,000.

The diversity of these publications is evident at a glance. Yet they can only faintly suggest the multitude of cleavages which exist in our society, and along which flow information and opinion carrying authority to the individual groups.

Here are the conventions scheduled for Cleveland, Ohio, recorded in a single recent issue of "World Convention Dates"—a fraction of the 5,500 conventions and rallies scheduled:

The Employing Photo-Engravers' Association of

America; The Outdoor Writers' Association; the Knights of St. John; the Walther League; The National Knitted Outerwear Association; The Knights of St. Joseph; The Royal Order of Sphinx; The Mortgage Bankers' Association; The International Association of Public Employment Officials; The Kiwanis Clubs of Ohio; The American Photo-Engravers' Association; The Cleveland Auto Manufacturers Show; The American Society of Heating and Ventilating Engineers.

Other conventions to be held in 1928 were those of: The Association of Limb Manufacturers' Association; The National Circus Fans' Association of America; The American Naturopathic Association; The American Trap Shooting Association; The Texas Folklore Association; The Hotel Greeters; The Fox Breeders' Association; The Insecticide and Disinfectant Association; The National Association of Egg Case and Egg Case Filler Manufacturers; The American Bottlers of Carbonated Beverages; and The National Pickle Packers' Association, not to mention the Terrapin Derby—most of them with banquets and orations attached.

If all these thousands of formal organizations and institutions could be listed (and no complete list has ever been made), they would still represent but a part of those existing less formally but leading vigorous lives. Ideas are sifted and opinions stereotyped in the neighborhood bridge club. Leaders assert their authority through community drives and amateur theatricals. Thousands of women may unconsciously belong to a sorority which follows the fashions set by a single society leader.

Life satirically expresses this idea in the reply which it represents an American as giving to the Britisher who praises this country for having no upper and lower classes or castes:

"Yeah, all we have is the Four Hundred, the WhiteCollar Men, Bootleggers, Wall Street Barons, Criminals, the D.A.R., the K.K.K., the Colonial Dames, the Masons, Kiwanis and Rotarians, the K. of C., the Elks, the Censors, the Cognoscenti, the Morons, Heroes Like Lindy, the W.C.T.U., Politicians, Menckenites, the Booboise, Immigrants, Broadcasters, and—the Rich and Poor."

Yet it must be remembered that these thousands of groups interlace. John Jones, besides being a Rotarian, is member of a church, a fraternal order, of a political party, of a charitable organization, of a professional association, of a local chamber of commerce, of a league for or against prohibition or of a society for or against lowering the tariff, or of a golf club. The opinions which he receives as a Rotarian, he will tend to disseminate in the other groups in which he may have influence.

This invisible, intertwining structure of groupings and associations is the mechanism by which democracy has organized its group mind and simplified its mass thinking. To deplore the existence of such a mechanism is to ask for a society such as never was and never will be. To admit that it exists, but expect that it shall not be used, is unreasonable.

Emil Ludwig represents Napoleon as "ever on the watch for indications of public opinion; always listening to the voice of the people, a voice which defies calculation. 'Do you know,' he said in those days, 'what amazes me more than all else? The impotence of force to organize anything.'"

It is the purpose of this book to explain the structure of the mechanism which controls the public mind, and to tell how it is manipulated by the special pleader who seeks to create public acceptance for a particular idea or commodity. It will attempt at the same time to find the due place in the modern democratic scheme for this new propaganda and to suggest its gradually evolving code of ethics and practice.

CHAPTER II

THE NEW PROPAGANDA

In the days when kings were kings, Louis XIV made his modest remark, "L'Etat c'est moi." He was nearly right.

But times have changed. The steam engine, the multiple press, and the public school, that trio of the industrial revolution, have taken the power away from kings and given it to the people. The people actually gained power which the king lost. For economic power tends to draw after it political power; and the history of the industrial revolution shows how that power passed from the king and the aristocracy to the bourgeoisie. Universal suffrage and universal schooling reinforced this tendency, and at last even the bourgeoisie stood in fear of the common people. For the masses promised to become king.

Today, however, a reaction has set in. The minority has discovered a powerful help in influencing majorities. It has been found possible to so mold the mind of the masses that they will throw their newly gained strength in the desired direction. In the present structure of society, this practice is inevitable. Whatever of social importance is done today, whether in politics, finance, manufacture, agriculture, charity, education, or other fields, must be done with the help of propaganda. Propaganda is the executive arm of the invisible government.

Universal literacy was supposed to educate the common man to control his environment. Once he could read and write he would have a mind fit to rule. So ran the democratic doctrine. But instead of a mind, universal literacy has given him rubber stamps, rubber stamps inked with advertising slogans, with editorials, with published scientific data, with the trivialities of the tabloids and the platitudes of history, but quite innocent of original thought. Each man's rubber stamps are the duplicates of millions of others, so that when those millions are exposed to the same stimuli, all received identical imprints. It may seem an exaggeration to say that the American public gets most of its ideas in this wholesale fashion. The mechanism by which ideas are disseminated on a large scale is propaganda, in the broad sense of an organized effort to spread a particular belief or doctrine.

I am aware that the word *propaganda* carries to many minds an unpleasant connotation. Yet whether, in any instance, propaganda is good or bad depends upon the merit of the cause urged, and the correctness of the information published.

In itself, the word *propaganda* has certain technical meanings which, like most things in this world, are "neither good nor bad but custom makes them so." I find the word defined in *Funk and Wagnall's Dictionary* in four ways:

"1. A society of cardinals, the overseers of foreign missions; also the College of Propaganda at Rome founded by Pope Urban VIII in 1627 for education of missionary priests; Sacred College de Propaganda Fide.

"2. Hence, any institution or scheme for propagating a doctrine or system.

"3. Effort directed systematically toward the gaining of public support for an opinion or a course of action.

"4. The principles advanced by a propaganda."

> The *Scientific American*, in a recent issue, pleads for the restoration to respectable usage of that "fine old word 'propaganda.'"
>
> "There is no word in the English language," it says, "whose meaning has been so sadly distorted as the word 'propaganda.' The change took place mainly during the late war when the term took on a decidedly sinister complexion."
>
> "If you turn to the Standard Dictionary, you will find that the word was applied to a congregation or society of cardinals for the care and oversight of foreign missions which was instituted at Rome in the year 1627. It was applied also to the College of the Propaganda at Rome that was founded by Pope Urban VIII, for the education of the missionary priests. Hence, in later years the word came to be applied to any institution or scheme for propagating a doctrine or system."
>
> "Judged by this definition, we can see that in its true sense propaganda is a perfectly legitimate form of human activity. Any society, whether it be social, religious or political, which is possessed of certain beliefs, and sets out to make them known,

either by the spoken or written words, is practicing propaganda."

"Truth is mighty and must prevail, and if any body of men believe that they have discovered a valuable truth, it is not merely their privilege but their duty to disseminate that truth. If they realize, as they quickly must, that this spreading of the truth can be done upon a large scale and effectively only by organized effort, they will make use of the press and the platform as the best means to give it wide circulation. Propaganda becomes vicious and reprehensive only when its authors consciously and deliberately disseminate what they know to be lies, or when they aim at effects which they know to be prejudicial to the common good."

"'Propaganda' in its proper meaning is a perfectly wholesome word, of honest parentage, and with an honorable history. The fact that it should today be carrying a sinister meaning merely shows how much of the child remains in the average adult. A group of citizens writes and talks in favor of a certain course of action in some debatable question, believing that it is promoting the best interest of the community. Propaganda? Not a bit of it. Just a plain forceful statement of truth. But let another group of citizens express opposing views, and they are promptly labeled with the sinister name of propaganda…"

"'What is sauce for the goose is sauce for gander,' says a wise old proverb. Let us make haste to put this fine old word back where it belongs, and restore its dignified significance for the use of our children and our children's children."

The extent to which propaganda shapes the progress of affairs about us may surprise even well informed persons.

Nevertheless, it is only necessary to look under the surface of the newspaper for a hint as to propaganda's authority over public opinion. Page one of the *New York Times* on the day these paragraphs are written contains eight important news stories. Four of them, or one-half, are propaganda. The casual reader accepts them as accounts of spontaneous happenings. But are they? Here are the headlines which announce them:

"TWELVE NATIONS WARN CHINA REAL REFORM MUST COME BEFORE THEY GIVE RELIEF,"

"PRITCHETT REPORTS ZIONISM WILL FAIL,"

"REALTY MEN DEMAND A TRANSIT INQUIRY,"

"OUR LIVING STANDARD HIGHEST IN HISTORY, SAYS HOOVER REPORT,"

Take them in order: The article on China explains the joint report of the Commission on Extraterritoriality in China, presenting an exposition of the Powers' stand in the Chinese muddle. What it says is less important than what it is. It was "made public by the State Department today" with the purpose of presenting to the American public a picture of the State Department's position. Its source gives it authority, and the American public tends to accept and support the State Department view.

The report of Dr. Pritchett, a trustee of the Carnegie Foundation for International Peace, is an attempt to find the facts about this Jewish colony in the midst of a restless Arab world. When Dr. Pritchett's survey convinced him that in the long run Zionism would "bring more bitterness and more unhappiness both for the Jew and for the Arab," this point of view was broadcast with all the authority of the Carnegie Foundation, so that the public would hear and believe. The statement by the president of the Real Estate Board of New York, and Secretary Hoover's report, are similar attempts to influence the public toward an opinion.

These examples are not given to create the impression that there is anything sinister about propaganda. They are set down rather to illustrate how conscious direction is given to events, and how the men behind these events influence public opinion. As such they are examples of modern propaganda. At this point we may attempt to define propaganda.

Modern propaganda is a consistent, enduring effort to create or shape events to influence the relations of the public to an enterprise, idea or group.

This practice of creating circumstances and of creating pictures in the minds of millions of persons is very common. Virtually no important undertaking is now carried on without it, whether the enterprise be building a cathedral, endowing a university, marketing a moving picture, floating a large bond issue, or electing a president. Sometimes the effect on the public is created by a professional propagandist, sometimes by an amateur deputed for the job. The important thing is that it is universal and continuous; and in its sum total it is regimenting the public mind every bit as much as an army regiments the bodies of its soldiers.

So vast are the numbers of minds which can be regimented, and so tenacious are they when regimented, that a group at times offers an irresistible pressure before which legislators, editors, and teachers are helpless. The group will cling to its stereotypes, as Walter Lippmann calls it, making of those supposedly powerful beings, the leaders of public opinion, mere bits of driftwood in the surf. When an Imperial Wizard, sensing what is perhaps hunger for an ideal, offers a picture of a nation all Nordic and nationalistic, the common man of the older American stock, feeling himself elbowed out of his rightful position and prosperity by the newer immigrant stocks, grasps the picture which fits in so neatly with his prejudices, and makes it his own. He buys the sheet and pillowcase costume, and bands with his fellows by the thousand into a huge group powerful enough to swing state elections and to throw a ponderous monkey wrench into a national convention.

In our present social organization approval of the public is essential to any large undertaking. Hence a laudable movement may be lost unless it impresses itself on the public mind. Charity, as well as business, and politics and literature, for that matter, have had to adopt propaganda, for the public must be regimented into giving money just as it must be regimented into tuberculosis prophylaxis. The Near East Relief, the Association for the Improvement of the Condition of the Poor of New York, and all the rest, have to work on public opinion just as though they had tubes of toothpaste to sell. We are proud of our diminishing infant death rate—and that too is the work of propaganda.

Propaganda does exist on all sides of us, and it does change our mental pictures of the world. Even if this be unduly pessimistic—and that remains to be proved—the opinion reflects a tendency that is undoubtedly real. In fact, its use is growing as its efficiency in gaining public support is recognized.

This then evidently indicates the fact that anyone with sufficient influence can lead sections of the public, at least for a time and for a given purpose. Formerly the rulers were the leaders. They laid out the course of history, by the simple process of doing what they wanted. And if nowadays the successors of the rulers, those whose position or ability gives them power, can no longer do what they want without the approval of the masses, they find in propaganda a tool which is increasingly powerful in gaining that approval. Therefore, propaganda is here to stay.

It was, of course, the astounding success of propaganda during the war that opened the eyes of the intelligent few in all departments of life to the possibilities of regimenting the public mind. The American government and numerous patriotic agencies developed a technique which, to most persons accustomed to bidding for public acceptance, was new. They not only appealed to the individual by means of every approach—visual, graphic, and auditory—to support the national endeavor, but they also secured the cooperation of the key men in every group—persons whose mere word carried authority to hundreds or thousands or hundreds of thousands of followers. They thus automatically gained the support of fraternal, religious, commercial, patriotic, social, and local groups whose members took their opinions from their accustomed leaders and spokesmen, or from the periodical publications which they were accustomed to read and believe. At the same time, the manipulators of patriotic opinion made use of the mental clichés and the emotional habits of the public to produce mass reactions against the alleged atrocities, the terror, and the tyranny of the enemy. It was only natural, after the war ended, that intelligent persons should ask themselves whether it was possible to apply a similar technique to the problems of peace.

As a matter of fact, the practice of propaganda since the war has assumed very different forms from those prevalent twenty years ago. This new technique may fairly be called the new propaganda.

It takes account not merely of the individual, nor even of the mass mind alone, but also and especially of the anatomy of society, with its interlocking group formations and loyalties. It sees the individual not only as a cell in the social organism but as a cell organized into the social unit. Touch a nerve at a sensitive spot and you get an automatic response from certain specific members of the organism.

Business offers graphic examples of the effect that may be produced upon the public by interested groups, such as textile manufacturers losing their markets. This problem arose, not long ago, when the velvet manufacturers were facing ruin because their product had long been out of fashion. Analysis showed that it was impossible to revive a velvet fashion within America. Anatomical hunt for the vital spot! Paris! Obviously! But yes and no. Paris is the home of fashion. Lyons is the home of silk. The attack had to be made at the source. It was determined to substitute purpose for chance and to utilize the regular sources for fashion distribution and to influence the public from these sources. A velvet fashion service, openly supported by the manufacturers, was organized. Its first function was to establish contact with the Lyons manufactories and the Paris couturiers to discover what they were doing, to encourage them to act on behalf of velvet, and to help in the proper exploitation of their wares. An intelligent Parisian was enlisted in the work. He visited Lanvin and Worth, Agnes and Patou, and others and induced them to use velvet in their gowns and hats. It was he who arranged for the distinguished Countess This or Duchess That to wear the hat or the gown. And as for the presentation of the idea to the public, the American buyer or the American woman of fashion was simply shown the velvet creations in the atelier of the dressmaker or the milliner. She bought the velvet because she liked it and because it was in fashion.

The editors of the American magazines and fashion reporters of the American newspapers likewise subjected to the actual (although created) circumstance, reflected it in their news, which, in turn, subjected the buyer and the consumer here to the same influences. The result was that what was at first a trickle of velvet became a flood. A demand was slowly, but deliberately, created in Paris and America. A big department store, aiming to be a style leader, advertised velvet gowns and hats on the authority of the French couturiers, and quoted original cables received from them. The echo of the new style was heard from hundreds of department stores throughout the country which wanted to be style leaders too. Bulletins followed dispatches. The mail followed the cables. And the American woman traveler appeared before the ship news photographers in velvet gown and hat.

The created circumstances had their effect. "Fickle fashion has veered to velvet," was one newspaper comment.

And the industry in the United States again kept thousands busy.

The new propaganda, having regard to the constitution of society as a whole, not infrequently serves to focus and realize the desires of the masses. A desire for a specific reform, however widespread, cannot be translated into action until it is made articulate, and until it has exerted sufficient pressure upon the proper law-making bodies. Millions of housewives may feel that manufactured foods deleterious to health should be prohibited. But there is little chance that their individual desires will be translated into effective legal form unless their half-expressed demand can be organized, made vocal, and concentrated upon the state legislature or upon the Federal Congress in some mode which will produce the results they desire. Whether they realize it or not, they call upon propaganda to organize and effectuate their demand.

But clearly it is the intelligent minorities which need to make use of propaganda continuously and systematically. In the active proselytizing minorities in whom selfish interests and public interests coincide lie the progress and development of America. Only through the active energy of the intelligent few can the public at large become aware of and act upon new ideas.

Small groups of persons can, and do, make the rest of us think what they please about a given subject. But there are usually proponents and opponents of every propaganda, both of whom are equally eager to convince the majority.

CHAPTER III

THE NEW PROPAGANDISTS

Who are the men, who, without our realizing it, give us our ideas, tell us whom to admire and whom to despise, what to believe about the ownership of public utilities, about the tariff, about the price of rubber, about the Dawes Plan, about immigration; who tell us how our houses should be designed, what furniture we should put into them, what menus we should serve at our table, what kind of shirts we must wear, what sports we should indulge in, what plays we should see, what charities we should support, what pictures we should admire, what slang we should affect, what jokes we should laugh at?

If we set out to make a list of the men and women who, because of their position in public life, might fairly be called the molders of public opinion, we could quickly arrive at an extended list of persons mentioned in "Who's Who." It would obviously include the President of the United States and the members of his Cabinet; the Senators and Representatives in Congress; the Governors of the forty-eight states; the presidents of the chambers of commerce in our hundred largest cities, the chairmen of the boards of directors of our hundred or more largest industrial corporations, the president of many of the labor unions affiliated in the American Federation of Labor, the national president of each of the national professional and fraternal organizations, the president of each of the racial or language societies in the country, the hundred leading newspaper and magazine editors, the fifty most popular authors, the presidents of the fifty leading charitable organizations, the twenty leading theatrical or cinema producers, the hundred recognized leaders or fashion, the most popular and influential clergymen in the hundred leading cities, the presidents of our colleges and universities and the foremost members of their faculties, the most powerful financiers in Wall Street, the most noted amateurs of sports, and so on.

Such a list would comprise several thousand persons. But it is well known that many of these leaders are themselves led, sometimes by persons whose names are known to few. Many a congressman, in framing his platform, follows the suggestions of a district boss whom few persons outside the political machines have ever heard of. Eloquent divines may have great influence in their communities, but often take their doctrines from a higher ecclesiastical authority. The presidents of chambers of commerce mold the thought of local business men concerning public issues, but the opinions which they promulgate are usually derived from some national authority. A presidential candidate may be "drafted" in response to "overwhelming popular demand," but it is well known that his name may be decided upon by half a dozen men sitting around a table in a hotel room.

In some instances the power of invisible wirepullers is flagrant. The power of the invisible cabinet which deliberated at the poker table in a certain little green house in Washington has become a national legend. There was a period in which the major policies of the national government were dictated by a single man, Mark Hanna. A Simmons may, for a few years, succeed in marshaling millions of men on a platform of intolerance and violence.

Such persons typify in the public mind the type of ruler associated with the phrase *invisible government.* But we do not often stop to think that there are dictators in other fields whose influence is just as decisive as that of the politicians I have mentioned. Irene Castle can establish the fashion of short hair which dominates nine-tenths of the women who make any pretense to being fashionable. Paris fashion leaders set the mode of the short skirt, for wearing which, twenty years ago, any woman would simply have been arrested and thrown into jail by the New York City police; and the entire women's clothing industry, capitalized at hundreds of millions of dollars, must be reorganized to conform to their dictum.

There are invisible rulers who control the destinies of millions. It is not generally realized to what extent the words and actions of our most influential public men are dictated by shrewd persons operating behind the scenes.

Now, what is still more important, is the extent to which our thoughts and habits are modified by authorities.

In some departments of our daily life, in which we imagine ourselves free agents, we are ruled by dictators exercising great power. A man buying a suit of clothes imagines that he is choosing, according to his taste and his personality, the kind of garment which he prefers. In reality, he may be obeying the orders of an anonymous gentleman tailor in London. This personage is the silent partner in a modest tailoring establishment, which is patronized by gentlemen of fashion and princes of blood. He suggests to British noblemen and others a blue cloth instead of gray, two buttons instead of three, or sleeves a quarter of an inch narrower than last season. The distinguished customer approves of the idea.

But how does this fact affect John Smith of Topeka?

The gentleman tailor is under contract with a certain large American firm, which manufactures men's suits, to send them instantly the designs of the suits chosen by the leaders of London fashion. Upon receiving the designs, with specifications as to color, weight, and texture, the firm immediately places an order with the cloth makers for several hundred thousand dollars' worth of cloth. The suits made up according to the specifications are then advertised as the latest fashion. The fashionable men in New York Chicago, Boston, and Philadelphia wear them. And the Topeka man, recognizing this leadership, does the same.

Women are just as subject to the commands of invisible government as men. A silk manufacturer, seeking a new market for its product, suggested to a large manufacturer of shoes that women's shoes should be covered with silk to match their dresses. The idea was adopted and systematically propagandized. A popular actress was persuaded to wear the shoes. The fashion spread. The shoe firm was ready with the supply to meet the created demand. And the silk company was ready with the silk for more shoes.

The man who injected this idea into the shoe industry was ruling women in one department of their social lives. Different men rule us in the various departments of our lives. There may be one power behind the throne in politics, another in the manipulations of the Federal discount rate, and still another in the dictation of next season's dances. If there were a national invisible cabinet ruling our destinies (a thing which is not impossible to conceive of), it would work through certain group leaders on Tuesday for one purpose, and through an entirely different set on Wednesday for another. The idea of invisible government is relative. There may be a handful of men who control the educational methods of the great majority of our schools. Yet from another standpoint, every parent is a group leader with authority over his or her children.

The invisible government tends to be concentrated in the hands of the few because of the expense of manipulating the social machinery which controls the opinions and habits of the masses. To advertise on a scale which will reach fifty million persons is expensive. To reach and persuade the group leaders who dictate the public's thoughts and actions is likewise expensive.

For this reason there is an increasing tendency to concentrate the functions of propaganda in the hands of the propaganda specialist. This specialist is more and more assuming a distinct place and function in our natural life.

New activities call for new nomenclature. The propagandist who specializes in interpreting enterprises and ideas to the public, and in interpreting the public to promulgators of new enterprises and ideas, has come to be know by the name of "public relations counsel."

The new profession of public relations has grown up because of the increasing complexity of modern life and the consequent necessity for making the actions of one part of the public understandable to other sectors of the public. It is due, too, to the increasing dependence of organized power of all sorts upon public opinion. Governments, whether they are monarchical, constitutional, democratic or communist, depend upon acquiescent public opinion for the success of their efforts and, in fact, government is government only by virtue of public acquiescence. Industries, public utilities, educational movements, indeed all groups representing any concept or product, whether they are majority or minority ideas, succeed only because of approving public opinion. Public opinion is the unacknowledged partner in all broad efforts.

The public relations counsel, then, is the agent who, working with modern media of communications and the group formations of society, brings an idea to the consciousness of the public. But he is a great deal more than that. He is concerned with courses of action, doctrines, systems and opinions, and the securing of public support for them. He is also concerned with tangible things such as manufactured and raw products. He is concerned with public utilities, with large trade groups and associations representing entire industries.

He functions primarily as an adviser to his client, very much as a lawyer does. A lawyer concentrates on the legal aspects of his clients' business. A counsel on public relations concentrates on the public contacts of his client's business. Every phase of his client's ideas, products, or activities which may affect the public or in which the public may have an interest is part of his function.

For instance, in the specific problems of the manufacturer he examines the product, the markets, the way in which the public reacts to the product, the attitude of the employees to the public and towards the product, and the cooperation of the distribution agencies.

The counsel on public relations, after he has examined all these and other factors, endeavors to shape the actions of his client so that they will gain the interest, the approval, and the acceptance of the public.

The means by which the public is apprised of the actions of his client are as varied as the means of communication themselves, such as conversation, letters, the stage, the motion picture, the radio, the lecture platform, the magazine, the daily newspaper. The counsel on public relations is not an advertising man but he advocates advertising where that is indicated. Very often he is called in by an advertising agency to supplement its work on behalf of a client. His work and that of the advertising agency do not conflict with or duplicate each other.

His first efforts are, naturally, devoted to analyzing his clients' problems, and making sure that what he has to offer the public is something which the public accepts or can be brought to accept. It is futile to attempt to sell an idea or to prepare the ground for a product that is basically unsound.

For example, an orphan asylum is worried by a falling off in contributions and a puzzling attitude of indifference or hostility on the part of the public. The counsel on public relations may discover upon analysis that the public, alive to modern sociological trends, subconsciously criticizes the institution because it is not organized on the new "cottage plan." He will advise modification of the client in this respect. Or a railroad may be urged to put on a fast train for the sake of the prestige which it will lend to the road's name, and hence to its stocks and bonds.

If the corset makers, for instance, wished to bring the product into fashion again, he would unquestionably advise that the plan was impossible, since women have definitely emancipated themselves from the old-style corset. Yet his fashion advisers might report that women might be persuaded to adopt a certain type of girdle which eliminated the unhealthful features of the corset.

His next effort is to analyze his public. He studies the groups which must be reached, and the leaders through whom he may approach these groups. Social groups, economic groups, geographical groups, age groups, doctrinal groups, language groups, cultural groups, all these represent his divisions through which, on behalf of his client, he may talk to the public.

Only after this double analysis has been made and the results collated, has the time come for the next step, the formulation of policies governing the general practice, procedure, and habits of the client in all those aspects in which he comes in contact with the public. And only when these policies have been agreed upon is it time for the fourth step.

The first recognition of the distinct functions of the public relations counsel arose, perhaps, in the early years of the present century as a result of the insurance scandals coincident with the muckraking of corporate finance in the popular magazines. The interests thus attacked suddenly realized that they were completely out of touch with the public they were professing to serve, and required expert advice to show them how they could understand the public and interpret themselves to it.

The Metropolitan Life Insurance Company, prompted by the most fundamental self-interest, initiated a conscious, directed effort to change the attitude of the public toward insurance companies in general, and toward itself in particular, to its profit and the public's benefit.

It tried to make a majority movement of itself by getting the public to buy its policies. It reached the public at every point of its corporate and separate existences. To communities it gave health surveys and expert counsel. To individuals it gave health creeds and advice. Even the building in which the corporation was located was made a picturesque landmark to see and remember, in other words to carry on the associative process. And so this company came to have a broad general acceptance. The number and amount of its policies grew constantly, as its broad contacts with society increased.

Within a decade, many large corporations were employing public relations counsel under one title or another, for they had come to recognize that they depended upon public good will for their continued prosperity. It was no longer true that it was "none of the public's business" how the affairs of a corporation were managed. They were obliged to convince the public that they were conforming to its demands as to honesty and fairness. Thus a corporation might discover that its labor policy was causing public resentment, and might introduce a more enlightened policy solely for the sake of general good will. Or a department store, hunting for the cause of diminishing sales, might discover that its clerks had a reputation for bad manners, and initiate formal instruction in courtesy and tact.

The public relations expert may be known as public relations director or counsel. Often he is called secretary or vice president or director. Sometimes he is known as cabinet officer or commissioner. By whatever title he may be called, his function is well defined and his advice has definite bearing on the conduct of the group or individual with whom he is working.

Many persons still believe that the public relations counsel is a propagandist and nothing else. But, on the contrary, the stage at which many suppose he starts his activities may actually be the stage at which he ends them. After the public and the client are thoroughly analyzed and policies have been formulated, his work may be finished. In other cases the work of the public relations counsel must be continuous to be effective. For in many instances only by a careful system of constant, thorough and frank information will the public understand and appreciate the value of what a merchant, educator or statesman is doing. The counsel on public relations must maintain constant vigilance, because inadequate information, or false information from unknown sources, may have results of enormous importance. A single false rumor at a critical moment may drive down the price of a corporation's stock, causing a loss of millions to stockholders. An air of secrecy or mystery about a corporation's financial dealings may breed a general suspicion capable of acting as an invisible drag on the company's whole dealings with the public. The counsel on public relations must be in a position to deal effectively with rumors and suspicions, attempting to stop them at their source, counteracting them promptly with correct or more complete information through channels which will be most effective, or best of all establish such relationships of confidence in the concern's integrity that rumors and suspicions will have no opportunity to take root.

His function may include the discovery of new markets, the existence of which had been unsuspected.

If we accept public relations as a profession, we must also expect it to have ideals and ethics. The ideal of the profession is a pragmatic one. It is to make the producer, whether that producer be a legislature making laws or a manufacturer making a commercial product, understand what the public wants and to make the public understand the objectives of the producer. In relation to industry, the ideal of the profession is to eliminate the waste and the friction of that result when industry does things or makes things which its public does not want, or when the public does not understand what is being offered it. For example, the telephone companies maintain extensive public relations departments to explain what they are doing, so that energy may not be burned up in the friction of misunderstanding. A detailed description, for example, of the immense and scientific care which the company takes to choose clearly understandable and distinguishable exchange names, helps the public to appreciate the effort that is being made to give good service, and stimulates it to cooperate by enunciating clearly. It aims to bring about an understanding between educators and educated, between government and people, between charitable institutions and contributors, between nation and nation.

The profession of public relations counsel is developing for itself an ethical code which compares favorably with that governing the legal and medical professions. In part, this code is forced upon the public relations counsel by the very conditions of his work. While recognizing, just as the lawyer does, that everyone has the right to present his case in its best light, he nevertheless refuses a client whom he believes to be dishonest, a product which he believes to be fraudulent, or a cause which he believes to be antisocial.

One reason for this is that, even though a special pleader, he is not dissociated from the client in the public's mind. Another reason is that while he is pleading before the court—the court of public opinion—he is at the same time trying to affect that court's judgments and actions. In law, the judge and jury hold the deciding balance of power. In public opinion, the public relations counsel is judge and jury, because through his pleading of a case the public may accede his opinion and judgment.

He does not accept a client whose interests conflict with those of another client. He does not accept a client whose case he believes to be hopeless or whose product he believes to be unmarketable.

He should be candid in his dealings. It must be repeated that his business is not to fool or hoodwink the public. If he were to get such a reputations, his usefulness in his profession would be at an end. When he is sending out propaganda material, it is clearly labeled as to the source. The editor knows from whom it comes and what its purpose is, and accepts or rejects it on its merits as news.

CHAPTER IV

THE PSYCHOLOGY OF PUBLIC RELATIONS

The systematic study of mass psychology revealed to students the potentialities of invisible government of society by manipulation of the motives which actuate man in the group. Trotter and Le Bon, who approached the subject in a scientific manner, and Graham Wallas, Walter Lippmann, and others who continued with searching studies of the group mind, established that the group has mental characteristics distinct from those of the individual, and is motivated by impulses and emotions which cannot be explained on the basis of what we know of individual psychology. So the question naturally arose: If we understand the mechanism and motives of the group mind, is it not possible to control and regiment the masses according to our will without their knowing about it?

The recent practice of propaganda has proved that it is possible, at least up to a certain point and within certain limits. Mass psychology is as yet far from being an exact science and the mysteries of human motivation are by no means all revealed. But at least theory and practice have combined with sufficient success to permit us to know that in certain cases we can effect some change in public opinion with a fair degree of accuracy by operating a certain mechanism, jut as the motorist can regulate the speed of his car by manipulating the flow of gasoline. Propaganda is not a science in the laboratory sense, but it is no longer entirely the empirical affair that it was before the advent of the study of mass psychology. It is now scientific in the sense that it seeks to base its operations upon definite knowledge drawn from direct observation of the group mind, and upon the application of principles which have been demonstrated to be consistent and relatively constant.

The modern propagandist studies systematically and objectively the material with which he is working in the spirit of the laboratory. If the matter in hand is a nationwide sales campaign, he studies the field by means of a clipping service, or of a corps of scouts, or by personal study at a crucial spot. He determines, for example, which features of a product are losing their public appeal, and in what new direction the public taste is veering. He will not fail to investigate to what extent it is the wife who has the final word in the choice of her husband's car, or of his suits and shirts.

Scientific accuracy of results is not to be expected, because many of the elements of the situation must always be beyond his control. He may know with a fair degree of certainty that under favorable circumstances an international flight will produce a spirit of good will, making possible even the consummation of political programs. But he cannot be sure that some unexpected event will not overshadow this flight in the public interest, or that some other aviator may not do something more spectacular the day before. Even in his restricted field of public psychology there must always be a wide margin of error. Propaganda, like economics and sociology, can never be an exact science for the reason that its subject matter, like theirs, deals with human beings.

If you can influence the leaders, either with or without their conscious cooperation, you automatically influence the group which they sway. But men do not need to be actually gathered together in a public meeting or in a street riot to be subject to the influences of mass psychology. Because man is by nature gregarious he feels himself to be member of a herd, even when he is alone in his room with the curtains drawn. His mind retains the patterns which have been stamped on it by the group influences.

A man sits in his office deciding what stocks to buy. He imagines, no doubt, that he is planning his purchases according to his own judgment. In actual fact his judgment is a mélange of impressions stamped on his mind by outside influences which unconsciously control his thought. He buys a certain railroad stock because it was in the headlines yesterday and hence it is the one which comes most prominently to his mind; because he has a pleasant recollection of a good dinner on one of its fast trains; because it has a liberal labor policy, a reputation for honesty; because he has been told that J. P. Morgan owns some of its shares.

Trotter and Le Bon concluded that the group mind does not *think* in the strict sense of the word. In place of thoughts it has impulses, habits, and emotions. In making up its mind, its first impulse is usually to follow the example of a trusted leader. This is one of the most firmly established principles of mass psychology. It operates in establishing the rising or diminishing prestige of a summer resort, in causing a run on a bank, or a panic on the stock exchange, in creating a best-seller, or a box-office success.

But when the example of the leader is not at hand and the herd must think for itself, it does so by means of clichés, pat words or images which stand for a whole group of ideas or experiences. Not many years ago, it was only necessary to tag a political candidate with the word *interests* to stampede millions of people into voting against him, because anything associated with "the interests" seemed necessarily corrupt. Recently the word *Bolshevik* has performed a similar service for persons who wished to frighten the public away from a line of action.

By playing upon an old cliché, or manipulating a new one, the propagandist can sometimes swing a whole mass of group emotions. In Great Britain, during the war, the evacuation hospitals came in for a considerable amount of criticism because of the summary way in which they handled their wounded. It was assumed by the public that a hospital gives prolonged and conscientious attention to its patients. When the name was changed to evacuation posts, the critical reaction vanished. No one expected more than an adequate emergency treatment from an institution so named. The cliché *hospital* was indelibly associated in the public mind with a certain picture. To persuade the public to discriminate between one type of hospital and another, to dissociate the cliché from the picture it evoked, would have been an impossible task. Instead, a new cliché automatically conditioned the public emotion toward these hospitals.

Men are rarely aware of the real reasons which motivate their actions. A man may believe that he buys a motor car because, after careful study of the technical features of all makes on the market, he has concluded that this is the best. He is almost certainly fooling himself. He bought it, perhaps, because a friend whose financial acumen he respects bought one last week; or because his neighbors believed he was not able to afford a car of that class; or because its colors are those of his college fraternity.

It is chiefly the psychologists of the school of Freud who have pointed out that many of man's thoughts and actions are compensatory substitutes for desires which he has been obliged to suppress. A thing may be desired not for its intrinsic worth or usefulness, but because he has unconsciously come to see in it a symbol of something else, the desire for which he is ashamed to admit to himself. A man buying a car may think he wants it for purposes of locomotion, whereas the fact may be that he would really prefer not to be burdened with it, and would rather walk for the sake of his health. He may really want it because it is a symbol of social position, an evidence of his success in business, or a means of pleasing his wife.

This general principle, that men are very largely actuated by motives which they conceal from themselves, is as true of mass as of individual psychology. It is evident that the successful propagandist must understand the true motives and not be content to accept the reasons which men give for what they do.

It is not sufficient to understand only the mechanical structure of society, the groupings and cleavages and loyalties. An engineer may know all about the cylinders and pistons of a locomotive, but unless he knows how steam behaves under pressure he cannot make his engine run. Human desires are the steam which makes the social machine work. Only by understanding them can the propagandist control that vast, loose-jointed mechanism which is modern society.

The old propagandist based his work on the mechanistic reaction psychology then in vogue in our colleges. This assumed that the human mind was merely an individual machine, a system of nerves and nerve centers, reacting with mechanical regularity to stimuli, like a helpless, willless automaton. It was the special pleader's function to provide the stimulus which would cause the desired reaction in the individual purchaser.

It was one of the doctrines of the reaction psychology that a certain stimulus often repeated would create a habit, or that the mere reiteration of an idea would create a conviction. Suppose the old type of salesmanship, acting for a meat packer, was seeking to increase the sale of bacon. It would reiterate innumerable times in full-page advertisements: "Eat more bacon. Eat bacon because it is cheap, because it is good, because it gives you reserve energy."

The newer salesmanship, understanding the group structure of society and principles of mass psychology, would first ask: "Who is it that influences the eating habits of the world?" The answer, obviously, is: "The physicians." The new salesman will then suggest to physicians to say publicly that it is wholesome to eat bacon. He knows as a mathematical certainty that large numbers of persons will follow the advice of their doctors, because he understands the psychological relation of dependence of men upon their physicians.

The old-fashioned propagandist, using almost exclusively the appeal of the printed word, tried to persuade the individual reader to buy a definite article, immediately.

This approach is exemplified in a type of advertisement which used to be considered ideal from the point of view of directness and effectiveness:

"YOU (perhaps with a finger pointing at the reader) *buy O'Leary's rubber heels*—NOW."

The advertiser sought by means of reiteration and emphasis directed upon the individual to break down or penetrate sales resistance. Although the appeal was aimed at fifty million persons, it was aimed at each as an individual.

The new salesmanship has found it possible, by dealing with men in the mass through their group formations, to set up psychological and emotional currents which will work for him. Instead of assaulting sales resistance by direct attack, he is interested in removing sales resistance. He creates circumstances which will swing emotional currents so as to make for purchaser demand.

If, for instance, I want to sell pianos, it is not sufficient to blanket the country with a direct appeal, such as:

"YOU *buy a Mozart piano now. It is cheap. The best artists use it. It will last for years.*"

The claims may all be true, but they are in direct conflict with the claims of other piano manufacturers, and in indirect competition with the claims of a radio or a motorcar, each competing for the consumer's dollar.

What are the true reasons the purchaser is planning to spend his money on a new car instead of on a new piano? Because he has decided that he wants the commodity called locomotion more than he wants the commodity called music? Not altogether. He buys a car because it is at the moment the group custom to buy cars.

The modern propagandist therefore sets to work to

create circumstances which will modify that custom. He appeals perhaps to the home instinct which is fundamental. He will endeavor to develop public acceptance of the idea of a music room in the home. This he may do, for example, by organizing an exhibition of period music rooms designed by well-known decorators who themselves exert an influence on the buying groups. He enhances the effectiveness and prestige of these rooms by putting in them rare and valuable tapestries. Then, in order to create dramatic interest in the exhibit, he stages an event or ceremony. To this ceremony key people, persons known to influence the buying habits of the public, such as a famous violinist, a popular artist, and a society leader, are invited. These key people affect other groups, lifting the idea of the music room to a place in the public consciousness which it did not have before. The juxtaposition of these leaders, and the idea which they are dramatizing, are then projected to the wider public through various publicity channels. Meanwhile, influential architects have been persuaded to make the music room an integral architectural part of their plans with perhaps a specially charming niche in one corner for the piano. Less influential architects will as a matter of course imitate what is done by the men whom they consider masters of their profession. They in turn will implant the idea of the music room in the mind of the general public.

The music room will be accepted because it has been made the thing. And the man or woman who has a music room, or has arranged a corner of the parlor as a musical corner, will naturally think of buying a piano. It will come to him as his own idea.

Under the old salesmanship the manufacturer said

to the prospective purchaser, "Please buy a piano." The new salesmanship has reversed the process and caused the prospective purchaser to say to the manufacturer, "Please sell me a piano."

The value of the associative process in propaganda is shown in connection with a large real estate development. To emphasize that Jackson Heights was socially desirable, every attempt was made to produce this associative process. A benefit performance of the Jitney Players was staged for the benefit of earthquake victims of Japan, under the auspices of Mrs. Astor and others. The social advantages of the place were projected—a golf course was laid out and a clubhouse planned. When the post office was opened, the public relations counsel attempted to use it as a focus for national interest and discovered that its opening fell coincident with a date important in the annals of the American Postal Service. This was then made the basis of the opening.

When an attempt was made to show the public the beauty of the apartments, a competition was held among interior decorators for the best furnished apartment in Jackson Heights. An important committee of judges decided. This competition drew the approval of well-known authorities, as well as the interest of millions, who were made cognizant of it through newspaper and magazine and other publicity, with the effect of building up definitely the prestige of the development.

One of the most effective methods is the utilization of the group formation of modern society in order to spread ideas. An example of this is the nationwide competitions for sculpture in Ivory soap, open to school children in certain age groups as well as professional sculptors. A sculptor of national reputation found Ivory soap an excellent medium for sculpture.

The Procter and Gamble Company offered a series of prizes for the best sculpture in white soap. The contest was held under the auspices of the Art Center in New York City, an organization of high standing in the art world.

School superintendents and teachers throughout the country were glad to encourage the movement as an educational aid for schools. Practice among school children as part of their art courses was stimulated. Contests were held between schools, between school districts and cities.

Ivory soap was adaptable for sculpturing in the homes because mothers saved the shavings and the imperfect efforts for laundry purposes. The work itself was clean.

The best pieces are selected from the local competitions for entry in the national contest. This is held annually at an important art gallery in New York, whose prestige with that of the distinguished judges, establishes the contest as a serious art event.

In the first of these national competitions about 500 pieces of sculpture were entered. In the third, 2,500. And in the fourth, more than 4,000. If the carefully selected pieces were so numerous, it is evident that a vast number were sculptured during the year, and that a much greater number must have been made for practice purposes. The good will was greatly enhanced by the fact that this soap had become not merely the concern of the housewife but also a matter of personal and intimate interest to her children.

A number of familiar psychological motives were set in motion in the carrying out of this campaign. The aesthetic, the competitive, the gregarious (much of the sculpturing was done in school groups), the snobbish (the impulse to follow the example of a recognized leader), the exhibitionist, and—last but by no means least—the maternal.

All these motives and group habits were put in concerted motion by the simple machinery of group leadership and authority. As if actuated by the pressure of a button, people began working for the sake of the gratification obtained in the sculpture work itself.

This point is most important in successful propaganda work. The leaders who lend their authority to any propaganda campaign will do so only if it can be made to touch their own interests. There must be a disinterested aspect of the propagandist's activities. In other words, it is one of the functions of the public relations counsel to discover at what points his client's interests coincide with those of other individuals or groups.

In the case of the soap sculpture competition, the distinguished artists and educators who sponsored the idea were glad to lend their services and their names because the competitions really promoted an interest which they had at heart—the cultivation of the aesthetic impulse among the younger generation.

Such coincidence and overlapping of interests is as infinite as the interlacing of group formations themselves. For example, a railway wishes to develop its business. The counsel on public relations makes a survey to discover at what points its interests coincide with those of its prospective customers. The company then establishes relations with chambers of commerce along its right of way and assists them in developing their communities. It helps them to secure new plants and industries for the town. It facilitates business through the dissemination of technical information. It is not merely a case of bestowing favors in the hope of receiving favors: these activities of the railroad, besides creating good will, actually promote growth on its right of way. The interests of the railroad and the communities through which it passes mutually interact and feed one another.

In the same way, a bank institutes an investment service for the benefit of its customers in order that the latter may have more money to deposit with the bank. Or a jewelry concern develops an insurance department to insure the jewels it sells, in order to make the purchaser feel greater security in buying jewels. Or a baking company establishes an information service suggesting recipes for bread to encourage new uses for bread in the home.

The ideas of the new propaganda are predicated on sound psychology based on enlightened self-interest.

I have tried, in these chapters, to explain the place of propaganda in modern American life and something of the methods by which it operates—to tell the why, the what, the who and the how of the invisible government which dictates our thoughts, directs our feelings, and controls our actions. In the following chapters I shall try to show how propaganda functions in specific departments of group activity, to suggest some of the further ways in which it may operate.

CHAPTER V

BUSINESS AND THE PUBLIC

The relationship between business and the public has become closer in the past few decades. Business today is taking the public into partnership. A number of causes, some economic, others due to the growing public understanding of business and the public interest in business, have produced this situation. Business realizes that its relationship to the public is not confined to the manufacture and sale of a given product, but includes at the same time the selling of itself and of all those things for which it stands in the public mind.

Twenty or twenty-five years ago, business sought to run its own affairs regardless of the public. The reaction was the muckracking period, in which a multitude of sins were, justly and unjustly, laid to the charge of the interests. In the face of an aroused public conscience the large corporations were obliged to renounce their contention that their affairs were nobody's business. If today big business were to seek to throttle the public, a new reaction similar to that of twenty years ago would take place and the public would rise and try to throttle big business with restrictive laws. Business is conscious of the public's conscience. This consciousness has led to a healthy cooperation.

Another cause for the increasing relationship is undoubtedly to be found in the various phenomena growing out of mass production. Mass production is profitable only if its rhythm can be maintained—that is, if it can continue to sell its product in steady or increasing quantity. The result is that while, under the handicraft of the small-unit system of production that was typical a century ago, demand created the supply, today supply must actively seek to create its corresponding demand. A single factory, potentially capable of supplying a whole continent with its particular product, cannot afford to wait until the public asks for its product; it must maintain constant touch, through advertising and propaganda, with the vast public in order to assure itself the continuous demand which alone will make its costly plant profitable. This entails a vastly more complex system of distribution than formerly. To make customers is the new problem. One must understand not only his own business—the manufacture of a particular product—but also the structure, the personality, the prejudices, of a potentially universal public.

Still another reason is to be found in the improvements in the technique of advertising—as regards both the size of the public which can be reached by the printed word, and the methods of appeal. The growth of newspapers and magazines having a circulation of millions of copies, and the art of the modern advertising expert in making the printed message attractive and persuasive, have placed the business man in a personal relation with a vast and diversified public.

Another modern phenomenon, which influences the

general policy of business, is the new competition between certain firms and the remainder of the industry to which they belong. Another kind of competition is between whole industries, in their struggle for a share of the consumer's dollar. When, for example, a soap manufacturer claims that his product will preserve youth, he is obviously attempting to change the public's mode of thinking about soap in general—a thing of grave importance to the whole industry. Or when the metal furniture industry seeks to convince the public that it is more desirable to spend its money for metal furniture than for wood furniture, it is clearly seeking to alter the taste and standards of a whole generation. In either case, business is seeking to inject itself into the lives and customs of millions of persons.

Even in a basic sense, business is becoming dependent on public opinion. With the increasing volume and wider diffusion of wealth in America, thousands of persons now invest in industrial stocks. New stock or bond flotations, upon which an expanding business must depend for its success, can be effected only if the concern has understood how to gain the confidence and good will of the general public. Business must express itself and its entire corporate existence so that the public will understand and accept it. It must dramatize its personality and interpret its objectives in every particular in which it comes into contact with the community (or the nation) of which it is a part.

An oil corporation which truly understands its manysided relation to the public will offer that public not only good oil but a sound labor policy. A bank will seek to show not only that its management is sound and conservative, but also that its officers are honorable both in their public and in their private life. A store specializing in fashionable men's clothing will express in its architecture the authenticity of the goods it offers. A bakery will seek to impress the public with the hygienic care observed in its manufacturing process, not only by wrapping its loaves in dust-proof paper and throwing its factory open to public inspection, but also by the cleanliness and attractiveness of its delivery wagons. A construction firm will take care that the public knows not only that its buildings are durable and safe, but also that its employees, when injured at work, are compensated. At whatever point a business enterprise impinges on the public consciousness, it must seek to give its public relations the particular character which will conform to the objectives which it is pursuing.

Just as the production manager must be familiar with every element and detail concerning the materials with which he is working, so the man in charge of a firm's public relations must be familiar with the structure, the prejudices, and the whims of the general public, and must handle his problems with the utmost care. The public has its own standards and demands and habits. You may modify them, but you dare not run counter to them. You cannot persuade a whole generation of women to wear long skirts, but you may, by working through leaders of fashion, persuade them to wear evening dresses which are long in back. The public is not an amorphous mass which can be molded at will, or dictated to. Both business and the public have their own personalities which must somehow be brought into friendly agreement. Conflict and suspicion are injurious to both. Modern business must study on what terms the partnership can be made amicable and mutually beneficial. It must explain itself, its aims, its objectives, to the public in terms which the public can understand and is willing to accept.

Business does not willingly accept dictation from the public. It should not expect that it can dictate to the public. While the public should appreciate the great economic benefit which business offers, thanks to mass production and scientific marketing, business should also appreciate that the public is becomingly increasingly discriminative in its standards and should seek to understand its demands and meet them. The relationship between business and the public can be healthy only if it is the relationship of give and take.

It is this condition and necessity which has created the need for a specialized field of public relations. Business now calls in the public relations counsel to advise it, to interpret its purpose to the public, and to suggest those modifications which may make it conform to the public demand.

The modifications then recommended to make the business conform to its objectives and to the public demand may concern the broadest matters of policy or the apparently most trivial details of execution. It might in one case be necessary to transform entirely the lines of goods sold to conform to changing public demands. In another case the trouble may be found to lie in such small matters as the dress of the clerks. A jewelry store may complain that its patronage is shrinking upwards because of its reputation for carrying high-priced goods; in this case the public relations counsel might suggest the featuring of medium-priced goods, even at a loss, not because the firm desires a large medium-price trade as such, but because out of a hundred medium-price customers acquired today a certain percentage will be well-to-do ten years from now. A department store which is seeking to gather in the high-class trade may be urged to employ college graduates as clerks or to engage well-known modern artists to design show-windows or special exhibits. A bank may be urged to open a Fifth Avenue branch, not because the actual business done on Fifth Avenue warrants the expense, but because a beautiful Fifth Avenue office correctly expresses the kind of appeal which it wishes to make to future depositors; and, viewed in this way, it may be as important that the doorman be polite, or that the floors be kept clean, and that the branch manager be an able financier. Yet the beneficial effect of this branch may be canceled if the wife of the president is involved in a scandal.

Big business studies every move which may express its true personality. It seeks to tell the public, in all appropriate ways, by the direct advertising message and by the subtlest aesthetic suggestion, the quality of the goods or services which it has to offer. A store which seeks a large sales volume in cheap goods will preach prices day in and day out, concentrating its whole appeal on the ways in which it can save money for its clients. But a store seeking a high margin of profit on individual sales would try to associate itself with the distinguished and the elegant, whether by an exhibition of old masters or through the social activities of the owner's wife.

The public relations activities of a business cannot be a protective coloring to hide its real aims. It is bad business as well as bad morals to feature exclusively a few high-class articles, when the main stock is of medium grade or cheap, for the general impression given is a false one. A sound public relations policy will not attempt to stampede the public with exaggerated claims and false pretenses, but to interpret the individual business vividly and truly through every avenue that leads to public opinion. The New York Central Railroad has for decades sought to appeal to the public not only on the basis of the speed and safety of its trains, but also on the basis of their elegance and comfort. It is appropriate that the corporation should have personified to the general public in the person of so suave and ingratiating a gentleman as Chauncey M. Depew—an ideal window dressing for such an enterprise.

While the concrete recommendations of the public relations counsel may vary infinitely according to individual circumstances, his general plan of work may be reduced to two types, which I might term *continuous interpretation* and *dramatization by high-spotting*. The two may be alternative or may be pursued concurrently.

Continuous interpretation is achieved by trying to control every approach to the public mind in such a manner that the public receives the desired impression, often without being conscious of it. High-spotting, on the other hand, vividly seizes the attention of the public and fixes it upon some detail or aspect which is typical of the entire enterprise. When a real estate corporation which is erecting a tall office building makes it ten feet taller than the highest skyscraper in existence, that is dramatization.

Which method is indicated, or whether both be indicated concurrently, can be determined only after a full study of objectives and specific possibilities.

Another interesting case of focusing public attention on the virtues of a product was shown in the case of gelatin. Its advantages in increasing the digestibility and nutritional value of milk were proven in the Mellon Institute of Industrial Research. The suggestion was made and carried out that to further this knowledge, gelatin be used by certain hospitals and school systems, to be tested out there. The favorable results of such tests were then projected to other leaders in the field with the result that they followed that group leadership and utilized gelatin for the scientific purposes which had been proven to be sound at the research institution. The idea carried momentum.

The tendency of big business is to get bigger. Through mergers and monopolies it is constantly increasing the number of persons with whom it is in direct contact. All this has intensified and multiplied the public relationships of business.

The responsibilities are of many kinds. There is a responsibility to the stockholders—numbering perhaps five persons or five hundred thousand—who have entrusted their money to the concern and have the right to know how the money is being used. A concern which is fully aware of its responsibility toward its stockholders will furnish them with frequent letters urging them to use the product in which their money is invested, and use their influence to promote its sale. It has a responsibility toward the dealer which it may express by inviting him, at its expense, to visit the home factory. It has a responsibility toward the industry as a whole which should restrain it from making exaggerated and unfair selling claims. It has a responsibility toward the retailer, and will see to it that its salesmen express the quality of the product which they have to sell. There is a responsibility toward the consumer, who is pressed by a clean and well managed factory, open to his inspection. And the general public, apart from its function as a potential consumer, is influenced in its attitude toward the concern by what it knows of that concern's financial dealings, its labor policy, even by the livableness of the houses in which its employees dwell. There is no detail too trivial to influence the public in a favorable or unfavorable sense. The personality of the president may be a matter of importance, for he perhaps dramatizes the whole concern to the public mind. It may be very important to what charities he contributes, in what civic societies he holds office. If he is a leader in his industry, the public may demand that he be a leader in his community.

The businessman has become a responsible member of the social group. It is not a question of ballyhoo, of creating a picturesque fiction for public consumption. It is merely a question of finding the appropriate modes of expressing the personality that is to be dramatized. Some business men can be their own best public relations counsel. But in the majority of cases, knowledge of the public mind and of the ways in which it will react to an appeal is a specialized function which must be undertaken by the professional expert.

Big business, I believe, is realizing this more and more. It is increasingly availing itself of the services of the specialist in public relations (whatever may be the title accorded him). And it is my conviction that as big business becomes bigger the need for expert manipulation of its innumerable contacts with the public will become greater.

One reason the public relations of a business are frequently placed in the hands of an outside expert, instead of being confided to an officer of the company, is the fact that the correct approach to a problem may be indirect. For example, when the luggage industry attempted to solve some of its problems by a public relations policy, it was realized that the attitude of railroads, of steamship companies, and of foreign government-owned railroads was an important factor in the handling of luggage.

If a railroad and a baggage man, for their own interest, can be educated to handle baggage with more facility and promptness, with less damage to the baggage, and less inconvenience to the passenger; if the steamship company lets down, in its own interests, its restrictions on luggage; if the foreign government eases up on its baggage costs and transportation in order to further tourist travel; then the luggage manufacturers will profit.

The problem then, to increase the sale of their luggage, was to have these and other forces come over to their point of view. Hence the public relations campaign was directed not to the public, who were the ultimate consumers, but to these other elements.

Also, if the luggage manufacturer can educate the general public on what to wear on trips and when to wear it, he may be increasing the sale of men's and women's clothing, but he will, at the same time, be increasing the sale of his luggage.

Propaganda, since it goes to basic causes, can very often be most effective through the manner of its introduction. A campaign against unhealthy cosmetics might be waged by fighting for a return to the wash-cloth and soap—a fight that very logically might be taken up by health officials all over the country, who would urge the return to the salutary and helpful wash-cloth and soap, instead of cosmetics.

The development of public opinion for a cause or line of socially constructive action may very often be the result of a desire on the party of the propagandist to meet successfully his own problem which the socially constructive cause would further. And by doing so he is actually fulfilling a social purpose in the broadest sense.

The soundness of a public relations policy was likewise shown in the case of a shoe manufacturer who made service shoes for patrolmen, firemen, letter carriers, and men in similar occupations. He realized that if he could make acceptable the idea that men in such work ought to be well-shod, he would sell more shoes and at the same time further the efficiency of the men.

He organized, as part of his business, a foot protection bureau. This bureau disseminated scientifically accurate information on the proper care of the feet, principles which the manufacturer had incorporated in the construction of the shoes. The result was that civic bodies, police chiefs, fire chiefs, and others interested in the welfare and comfort of their men, furthered the ideas his product stood for and the product itself, with the consequent effect that more of his shoes were sold more easily.

The application of this principle of a common denominator of interest between the object that is sold and the public good-will can be carried to infinite degrees.

"It matters not how much capital you may have, how fair the rates may be, how favorable the conditions of service, if you haven't behind you a sympathetic public opinion, you are bound to fail." This is the opinion of Samuel Insull, one of the foremost traction magnates of the country. And the late Judge Gary, of the United States Steel Corporation, expressed the same idea when he said: "Once you have the good will of the general public, you can go ahead in the work of constructive expansion. Too often many try to discount this vague and intangible element. That way lies destruction."

Public opinion is no longer inclined to be unfavorable to the large business merger. It resents the censorship of business by the Federal Trade Commission. It has broken down the anti-trust laws where it thinks they hinder economic development. It backs great trusts and mergers which it excoriated a decade ago. The government now permits large aggregations of producing and distributing units, as evidenced by mergers among railroads and other public utilities, because representative government reflects public opinion. Public opinion itself fosters the growth of mammoth industrial enterprises. In the opinion of millions of small investors, mergers and trusts are friendly giants and not ogres, because of the economies, mainly due to quantity production, which they have effected, and can pass on to the consumer.

This result has been, to a great extent, obtained by a deliberate use of propaganda in its broadest sense. It was obtained not only by modifying the opinion of the public, as the governments modified and marshaled the opinion of their publics during the war, but often by modifying the business concern itself. A cement company may work with road commissions gratuitously to maintain testing laboratories in order to ensure the best-quality roads to the public. A gas company maintains a free school of cookery.

But it would be rash and unreasonable to take it for granted that because public opinion has come over to the side of big business, it will always remain there. Only recently, Professor W. Z. Ripley of Harvard University, one of the foremost national authorities on business organization and practice, exposed certain aspects of big business which tended to undermine public confidence in large corporations. He pointed out that the stockholder's supposed voting power is often illusory; that annual financial statements are sometimes so brief and summary that to the man in the street they are downright misleading; that the extension of the system of non-voting shares often places the effective control of corporations and their finances in the hands of a small clique of stockholders; and that some corporations refuse to give out sufficient information to permit the public to know the true condition of the concern.

Furthermore, no matter how favorably disposed the public be toward big business in general, the utilities are always fair game for public discontent and need to maintain good will with the greatest care and watchfulness. These and other corporations of a semi-public character will always have to face a demand for government or municipal ownership if such attacks as those of Professor Ripley are continued and are, in the public's opinion, justified, unless conditions are changed and care is taken to maintain the contact with the public at all points of their corporate existence.

The public relations counsel should anticipate such trends of public opinion and advise on how to avert them, either by convincing the public that its fears or prejudices are unjustified, or in certain cases by modifying the action of the client to the extent necessary to remove the cause of complaint. In such a case public opinion might be surveyed and the points of irreducible opposition discovered.

The aspects of the situation which are susceptible of logical explanation; to what extent the criticism or prejudice is a habitual emotional reaction and what factors are dominated by accepted clichés, might be disclosed. In each instance he would advise some action or modification of policy calculated to make the readjustment.

While government ownership is in most instances only varyingly a remote possibility, public ownership of big business through the increasing popular investment in stocks and bonds, is becoming more and more a fact. The importance of public relations from this standpoint is to be judged by the fact that practically all prosperous corporations expect at some time to enlarge operations, and will need to float new stock or bond issues. The success of such issues depends upon the general record of the concern in the business world, and also upon the good will which it has been able to create in the general public. When the Victor Talking Machine Company was recently offered to the public, millions of dollars' worth of stock were sold overnight. On the other hand, there were certain companies which, although they were financially sound and commercially prosperous, would be unable to float a large stock issue, because public opinion is conscious of them, or has some unanalyzed prejudice against them.

To such an extent is the successful floating of stocks and bonds dependent upon the public favor that the success of a new merger may stand or fall upon the public acceptance which it is created for it. A merger may bring into existence huge new resources, and these resources, perhaps amounting to millions of dollars in a single operation, can often fairly be said to have been created by the expert manipulation of public opinion. It must be repeated that I am not speaking of artificial value given to a stock by dishonest propaganda or stock manipulation, but of the real economic values which are created when genuine public acceptance is gained for an industrial enterprise and becomes a real partner in it.

The growth of big business is so rapid that in some lines ownership is more international than national. It is necessary to reach ever larger groups of people if modern industry and commerce are to be financed. Americans have purchased billions of dollars of foreign industrial securities since the war, and Europeans own, it is estimated, between one and two billion dollars' worth of ours. In each case public acceptance must be obtained for the issue and the enterprise behind it.

Public loans, state or municipal, to foreign countries depend upon the good will which those countries have been able to create for themselves here. An attempted issue by an east European country is faring badly largely because of unfavorable public reaction to behavior of members of the ruling family. But other countries have no difficulty in placing any issue because the public is already convinced of the prosperity of these nations and the stability of their governments.

The new technique of public relations counsel is serving a very useful purpose in business by acting as a complement to legitimate advertisers and advertising in helping to break down unfair competitive exaggerated and overemphatic advertising by reaching the public with the truth through other channels than advertising. Where two competitors in a field are fighting each other with this type of advertising, they are undermining that particular industry to a point where the public may lose confidence in the whole industry. The only way to combat such unethical methods is for ethical members of the industry to use the weapon propaganda in order to bring out the basic truths of the situation.

Take the case of toothpaste, for instance. Here is a highly competitive field in which the preponderance of public acceptance of one product over another can very legitimately rest in inherent values. However, what has happened in this field?

One or two of the large manufacturers have asserted advantages for their toothpastes which no single toothpaste discovered up to the present time can possibly have. The competing manufacturer is put in the position either of overemphasizing an already exaggerated emphasis or of letting the overemphasis of his competitor take away his markets. He turns to the weapon of propaganda which can effectively, through various channels of approach to the public—the dental clinics, the schools, the women's clubs, the medical colleges, the dental press and even the daily press—bring to the public the truth of what a toothpaste can do. This will, of course, have its effect in making the honestly advertised toothpaste get to its real public.

Propaganda is potent in meeting unethical or unfair advertising. Effective advertising has become more costly than ever before. Years ago, when the country was smaller and there was no tremendous advertising machinery, it was comparatively easy to get country-wide recognition for a product. A corps of traveling salesmen might persuade the retailers, with a few cigars and a repertory of funny stories, to display and recommend their article on a nationwide scale. Today, a small industry is swamped unless it can find appropriate and relatively inexpensive means of making known the special virtues of its product, while larger industries have sought to overcome the difficulty by cooperative advertising, in which associations of industries compete with other associations.

Mass advertising has produced new kinds of competition. Competition between rival products in the same line is, of course, as old as economic life itself. In recent years much has been said of the new competition; we have discussed it in a previous chapter, between one group of products and another. Stone competes against wood for building; linoleum against carpets; oranges against apples; tin against asbestos for roofing.

This type of competition has been humorously illustrated by Mr. O. H. Cheney, Vice President of the American Exchange and Irving Trust Company of New York, in a speech before the Chicago Business Forum.

"Do you represent the millinery trades?" said Mr. Cheney. "The man at your side may serve the fur industry, and by promoting the style of big fur collars on women's coats he is ruining the hat business by forcing women to wear small and inexpensive hats. You may be interested in the ankles of the fair sex—I mean, you may represent the silk hosiery industry. You have two brave rivals who are ready to fight to the death—to spend millions in the fight—for the glory of those ankles—the leather industry, which has suffered from the low-show vogue, and the fabrics manufacturers, who yearn for the good old days when skirts were skirts.

"If you represent the plumbing and heating business, you are the mortal enemy of the textile industry, because warmer homes mean lighter clothes. If you represent the printers, how can you shake hands with the radio equipment man?...

"These are really only obvious forms of what I have called the new competition. The old competition was that between the members of each trade organization. One phase of the new competition is that between the trade associations themselves—between you gentlemen who represent those industries. Inter-commodity competition is the new competition between products used alternatively for the same purpose. Inter-industrial competition is the new competition between apparently unrelated industries which affect each other or between such industries as compete for the consumer's dollar—and that means practically all industries…

"Inter-commodity competition is, of course, the most spectacular of all. It is the one which seems most of all to have caught the business imagination of the country. More and more businessmen are beginning to appreciate what inter-commodity competition means to them. More and more they are calling upon their trade associations to help them—because inter-commodity competition cannot be fought single-handed.

"Take the great war on the dining-room table, for instance. Three times a day practically every dining room table in the country is the scene of a fierce battle in the competition. Shall we have prunes for breakfast? No, cry the embattled orange-growers and the massed legions of pineapple canners. Shall we eat sauerkraut? Why not eat green olives? is the answer of the Spaniards. Eat macaroni as a change from potatoes, says one advertiser—and will the potato growers take this challenge lying down?

"The doctors and dietitians tell us that a normal hardworking man needs only about two or three thousand calories of food a day. A banker, I suppose, needs a little less. But what am I to do? The fruit growers, the wheat raisers, the meat packers, the milk producers, the fishermen—all want me to eat more of their products—and are spending millions of dollars a year to convince me. Am I to eat to the point of exhaustion, or am I to obey the doctor and let the farmer and the food packers and the retailer go broke! Am I to balance my diet in proportion to the advertising appropriations of the various producers? Or am I to balance my diet scientifically and let those who overproduce go bankrupt? The new competition is probably keenest in the food industries because we have a very real limitation on what we can consume—in spite of higher incomes and higher living standards, we cannot eat more than we can eat."

I believe that competition in the future will not be only an advertising competition between individual products or between big associations, but that it will in addition be a competition of propaganda. The businessman and advertising man is realizing that he must not discard entirely the methods of Barnum in reaching the public. An example in the annuals of George Harrison Phelps, of the successful utilization of this type of appeal was the nationwide hook-up which announced the launching of the Dodge Victory Six Car.

Millions of people, it is estimated, listened in to this programs broadcast over forty-seven stations. The expense was more than $60,000. The arrangements involved an additional telephonic hookup of 20,000 miles of wire, and included transmission from Los Angeles, Chicago, Detroit, New Orleans, and New York. Al Jolson did his bit from New Orleans, Will Rogers from Beverly

Hills, Fred and Dorothy Stone from Chicago, and Paul Whiteman from New York, at an aggregate artists' fee of $25,000. And there was included a four-minute address by the president of Dodge Brothers announcing the new car, which gave him access in four minutes to an estimated audience of thirty million Americans, the largest number, unquestionably, ever to concentrate their attention on a given commercial product at a given moment. It was a sugar-coated sales message.

Modern sales technicians will object: "What you say of this method of appeal is true. But it increases the cost of getting the manufacturer's message across. The modern tendency has been to reduce this cost (for example, the elimination of premiums) and concentrate on getting full efficiency from the advertising expenditure. If you hire a Galli-Curci to sing for bacon you increase the cost of the bacon by the amount of her very large fee. Her voice adds nothing to the product but it adds to its cost."

Undoubtedly. But all modes of sales appeal require the spending of money to make the appeal attractive. The advertiser in print adds to the cost of his message by the use of pictures or by the cost of getting distinguished endorsements.

There is another kind of difficulty, created in the process of big business getting bigger, which calls for new modes of establishing contact with the public. Quantity production offers a standardized product the cost of which tends to diminish with the quantity sold. If low price is the only basis of competition with rival products, similarly produced, there ensues a cut-throat competition which can end only by taking all the profit and incentive out of the industry.

The logical way out of this dilemma is for the manufacturer to develop some sales appeal other than mere cheapness, to give the product, in the public mind, some other attraction, some idea that will modify the product slightly, some element of originality that will distinguish it from products in the same line. Thus, a manufacturer of typewriters paints his machines in cheerful hues. These special types of appeal can be popularized by the manipulation of the principles familiar to the propagandist—the principles of gregariousness, obedience to authority, emulation, and the like. A minor element can be made to assume economic importance by being established in the public mind as a matter of style. Mass production can be split up. Big business will still leave room for small business. Next to a huge department store there may be located a tiny specialty shop which makes a very good living.

The problem of bringing large hats back into fashion was undertaken by a propagandist. The millinery industry two years ago was menaced by the prevalence of the simple felt hat which was crowding out the manufacture of all other kinds of hats and hat ornaments. It was found that hats could roughly be classified in six types. It was found too that four groups might help to change hat fashions: the society leader, the style expert, the fashion editor and writer, the artist who might give artistic approval to the styles, and beautiful mannequins. The problem, then, was to bring these groups together before an audience of hat buyers.

A committee of prominent artists was organized to choose the most beautiful girls in New York to wear, in a series of tableaux, the most beautiful hats in the style classifications, at a fashion fête at a leading hotel.

A committee was formed of distinguished American women who, on the basis of their interest in the development of an American industry, were willing to add the authority of their names to the idea. A style committee was formed of editors of fashion magazines and other prominent fashion authorities who were willing to support the idea. The girls in their lovely hats and costumes paraded on the running-board before an audience of the entire trade.

The news of the event affected the buying habits not only of the onlookers, but also of the women throughout the country. The story of the event was flashed to the consumer by her newspaper as well as by the advertisements of her favorite store. Broadsides went to the millinery buyer from the manufacturer. One manufacturer stated that whereas before the show he had not sold any large trimmed hats, after it he had sold thousands.

Often the public relations man is called in to handle an emergency situation. A false rumor, for instance, may occasion an enormous loss in prestige and money if not handled promptly and effectively.

An incident such as the one described in the *New York American* of Friday, May 21, 1926, shows what the lack of proper technical handling of public relations might result in.

$1,000,000 LOST BY FALSE RUMOR ON HUDSON STOCK

Hudson Motor Company stock fluctuated widely around noon yesterday and losses estimated at $500,000 to $1,000,000 were suffered as a result of the widespread flotation of false news regarding dividend action.

The directors met in Detroit at 12:30, New York time, to act on a dividend. Almost immediately a false report that only the regular dividend had been declared was circulated.

At 12:46 the Dow, Jones & Co. ticker service received the report from the Stock Exchange firm and its publication resulted in further drop in the stock.

Shortly after 1 o'clock the ticker services received official news that the dividend had been increased and a 20 per cent stock distribution authorized. They rushed the correct news out on their tickers and Hudson stock immediately jumped more than 6 points.

A clipping from the *Journal of Commerce* of April 4, 1925 is reproduced here as an interesting example of a method to counteract a false rumor:

BEECH-NUT HEAD HOME TOWN GUEST
Bartlett Arkelly Signally Honored by
Communities of Mohawk Valley

(Special to the Journal of Commerce)

CANAJOHARIE, N.Y., April 3.—Today was 'Beech-Nut Day' in this town; in fact, for the Mohawk Valley. Business men and practically the whole community of this region joined in a personal testimonial to Bartlett Arkell of New York City,

> president of the Beech-Nut Packing Company of this city, in honor of his firm refusal to consider selling his company to other financial interests to move elsewhere.
>
> When Mr. Arkell publicly denied recent rumors that he was to sell his company to the Postum Cereal Company for $17,000,000, which would have resulted in taking the industry from its birthplace, he did so in terms conspicuously loyal to his boyhood home, which he has built up into a prosperous industrial community through thirty years' management of his Beech-Nut Company.
>
> He absolutely controls the business and flatly stated that he would never sell it during his lifetime 'to any one at any price,' since it would be disloyal to his friends and fellow workers. And the whole Mohawk Valley spontaneously decided that such sprit deserved public recognition. Hence, today's festivities.
>
> More than 3,000 people participated, headed by a committee comprising W.J. Roser, chairman; B.F. Spraker, H.V. Bush, B.F. Diefendorf and J.H. Cook. They were backed by the Canajoharie and the Mohawk Valley Chambers of Business Men's Associations.

Of course, everyone realized after this that there was no truth in the rumor that the Beech-Nut Company was on the market. A denial would not have carried as much conviction.

Amusement, too, is a business—one of the largest in America. It was the amusement business—first the circus and the medicine show, then the theater—which taught the rudiments of advertising to industry and commerce. The latter adopted the ballyhoo of the show business. But under the stress of practical experience it adapted and refines these crude advertising methods to the precise ends it sought to obtain. The theater has, in its turn, learned from business, and has refined its publicity methods to the point where the old stentorian methods are in the discard.

The modern publicity director of a theater syndicate or a motion picture trust is a businessman, responsible for the security of tens or hundreds of millions of dollars of invested capital. He cannot afford to be a stunt artist or a freelance adventurer in publicity. He must know his public accurately and modify its thoughts and actions by means of the methods which the amusement world has learned from its old pupil, big business. As public knowledge increases and public taste improves, business must be ready to meet them halfway.

Modern business must have its finger continuously on the public pulse. It must understand the changes in the public mind and be prepared to interpret itself fairly and eloquently to changing opinion.

CHAPTER VI

PROPAGANDA AND POLITICAL LEADERSHIP

The great political problem in our modern democracy is how to induce our leaders to lead. The dogma that the voice of the people is the voice of God tends to make elected persons the will-less servants of their constituents. This is undoubtedly part cause of the political sterility of which certain American critics constantly complain.

No serious sociologist any longer believes that the voice of the people expresses any divine or specially wise and lofty idea. The voice of the people expresses the mind of the people, and that mind is made up for it by the group leaders in whom it believes and by those persons who understand the manipulation of public opinion. It is composed of inherited prejudices and symbols and clichés and verbal formulas supplied to them by the leaders.

Fortunately, the sincere and gifted politician is able, by the instrument of propaganda, to mold and form the will of the people.

Disraeli cynically expressed the dilemma, when he said: "I *must* follow the people. Am I not their leader?" He might have added: "I *must* lead the people. Am I not their servant?"

Unfortunately, the methods of our contemporary politicians, in dealing with the public, are as archaic and ineffective as the advertising methods of business in 1900 would be today. While politics was the first important department of American life to use propaganda on a large scale, it has been the slowest in modifying its propaganda methods to meet the changed conditions of the public mind. American business first learned from politics the methods of appealing to the broad public. But it continually improved those methods in the course of its competitive struggle, while politics clung to the old formulas.

The political apathy of the average voter, of which we hear so much, is undoubtedly due to the fact that the politician does not know how to meet the conditions of the public mind. He cannot dramatize himself and his platform in terms which have real meaning to the public. Acting on the fallacy that the leader must slavishly follow, he deprives his campaign of all dramatic interest. An automaton cannot arouse the public interest. A leader, a fighter, a dictator, can. But, given our present political conditions under which every office seeker must cater to the vote of the masses, the only means by which the born leader can lead is the expert use of propaganda.

Whether in the problem of getting elected to office or in the problem of interpreting and popularizing new issues, or in the problem of making the day-to-day administration of public affairs a vital part of the community life, the use of propaganda, carefully adjusted to the mentality of the masses, is an essential adjunct of political life. The successful businessman today apes the politician. He has adopted the glitter and the ballyhoo of the campaign. He has set up all the sideshows. He has annual dinners that are a compendium of speeches, flags, bombast, stateliness, pseudo-democracy slightly tinged with paternalism. On occasion he doles out honors to employees, much as the republic of classic times rewarded its worthy citizens.

But these are merely the sideshows, the drums, of big business, by which it builds up an image of public service, and of honorary service. This is but one of the methods by which business stimulates loyal enthusiasms on the part of directors, the workers, the stockholders and the consumer public. It is one of the methods by which big business performs its function of making and selling products to the public. The real work and campaign of business consists of intensive study of the public, the manufacture of products based on this study, and exhaustive use of every means of reaching the public.

Political campaigns today are all sideshows, all honors, all bombast, glitter, and speeches. These are for the most part unrelated to the main business of studying the public scientifically, of supplying the public with party, candidate, platform, and performance, and selling the public these ideas and products.

Politics was the first big business in America.Therefore there is a good deal of irony in the fact that business has learned everything that politics has to teach, but that politics has failed to learn very much from business methods of mass distribution of ideas and products.

Emily Newell Blair has recounted in the *Independent* a typical instance of the waste of effort and money in a political campaign, a week's speaking tour in which she herself took part. She estimates that on a five-day trip covering nearly a thousand miles, she and the United States Senator with whom she was making political speeches addressed no more than 1,105 persons whose votes might conceivably have been changed as a result of their efforts. The cost of this appeal to these voters she estimates (calculating the value of the time spent on a very moderate basis) as $15.27 for each vote which might have been changed as a result of the campaign.

This, she says, was a "drive for votes, just as an Ivory Soap advertising campaign is a drive for sales." But, she asks, "what would a company executive say to a sales manager who sent a high-priced speaker to describe his product to less than 1,200 people at a cost of $15.27 for each possible buyer?" She finds it "amazing that the very men who make their millions out of cleverly devised drives for soap and bonds and cars will turn around and give large contributions to be expended for vote-getting in an utterly inefficient and antiquated fashion."

It is, indeed, incomprehensible that politicians do not make use of the elaborate business methods that the industry has built up. Because a politician knows political strategy, can develop campaign issues, can devise strong planks for platforms and envisage broad policies, it does not follow that he can be given the responsibility of selling ideas to a public as large as that of the United States.

The politician understands the public. He knows what the public wants and what the public will accept. But the politician is not necessarily a general sales manager, a public relations counsel, or a man who knows how to secure mass distribution of ideas.

Obviously, an occasional political leader may be capable of combining every feature of leadership, just as in business there are certain brilliant industrial leaders who are financiers, factory directors, engineers, sales managers, and public relations counsel all rolled into one.

Big business is conducted on the principle that it must prepare its policies carefully, and that in selling an idea to the large buying public of America, it must proceed according to broad plans. The political strategist must do likewise. The entire campaign should be worked out according to broad basic plans. Platforms, planks, pledges, budgets, activities, personalities, must be as carefully studied, apportioned and used as they are when big business desires to get what it wants from the public.

The first step in a political campaign is to determine the objectives, and to express them exceedingly well in the current form—that is, as a platform. In devising the platform the leader should be sure that it is an honest platform. Campaign pledges and promises should not be lightly considered by the public, and they ought to carry something of the guarantee principle and money-back policy that an honorable business institution carries with the sale of its goods. The public has lost faith in campaign promotion work. It does not say that politicians are dishonorable, but it does say that campaign pledges are written on the sand. Here then is one fact of public opinion of which the party that wishes to be successful might well take cognizance.

To aid in the preparation of the platform there should be made as nearly scientific an analysis as possible of the public and of the needs of the public. A survey of public desires and demands would come to the aid of the political strategist whose business it is to make a proposed plan of the activities of the parties and its elected officials during the coming terms of office.

A big business that wants to sell a product to the public surveys and analyzes its market before it takes a single step either to make or to sell the product. If one section of the community is absolutely sold to the idea of this product, no money is wasted in reselling it to it. If, on the other hand, another section of the public is irrevocably committed to another product, no money is wasted on a lost cause. Very often the analysis is the cause of basic changes and improvements in the product itself, as well as an index of how it is to be presented. So carefully is this analysis of markets and sales made that when a company makes out its sales budget for the year, it subdivides the circulations of the various magazines and newspapers it uses in advertising and calculates with a fair degree of accuracy how many times a section of that population is subjected to the appeal of the company. It knows approximately to what extent a national campaign duplicates and repeats the emphasis of a local campaign of selling.

As in the business field, the expenses of the political campaign should be budgeted. A large business today knows exactly how much money it is going to spend on propaganda during the next year or years. It knows that a certain percentage of its gross receipts will be given over to advertising—newspaper, magazine, outdoor and poster; a certain percentage to circularization and sales promotion—such as house organs and dealer aids; and a certain percentage must go to the supervising salesmen who travel around the country to infuse extra stimulus in the local sales campaign.

A political campaign should be similarly budgeted. The first question which should be decided is the amount of money that should be raised for the campaign. This decision can be reached by a careful analysis of campaign costs. There is enough precedent in business procedure to enable experts to work this out accurately. Then the second question of importance is the manner in which money should be raised.

It is obvious that politics would gain much in prestige if the money-raising campaign were conducted candidly and publicly, like the campaigns for the war funds. Charity drives might be made excellent models for political fund drives. The elimination of the little black bag element in politics would raise the entire prestige of politics in America, and the public interest would be infinitely greater if the actual participation occurred earlier and more constructively in the campaign.

Again, as in the business field, there should be a clear decision as to how the money is to be spent. This should be done according to the most careful and exact budgeting, wherein every step in the campaign is given its proportionate importance and the funds allotted accordingly. Advertising in newspapers and periodicals, posters and street banners, the exploitation of personalities in motion pictures, in speeches and lecturers and meetings, spectacular events and all forms of propaganda should be considered proportionately according to the budget, and should always be coordinated with the whole plan. Certain expenditures may be warranted if they represent a small proportion of the budget and may be totally unwarranted if they make up a large proportion of the budget.

In the same way the emotions by which the public is appealed to may be made part of the broad plan of the campaign. Unrelated emotions become maudlin and sentimental too easily, are often costly, and too often waste effort because the idea is not part of the conscious and coherent whole.

Big business has realized that it must use as many of the basic emotions as possible. The politician, however, has used the emotions aroused by words exclusively.

To appeal to the emotions of public in a political campaign is sound—in fact it is an indispensable part of the campaign. But the emotional content must:

(a) coincide in every way with the broad basic plans of the campaign and all its minor details;
(b) be adapted to the many groups of the public at which it is to be aimed; and
(c) conform to the media of the distribution of ideas.

The emotions of oratory have been worn down through long years of overuse. Parades, mass meetings, and the like are successful when the public has a frenzied emotional interest in the event. The candidate who takes babies on his lap, and has his photograph taken, is doing a wise thing emotionally, if this act epitomizes a definite plank in his platform. Kissing babies, if it's worth anything, must be used as a symbol for a baby policy and it must be synchronized with a plank in the platform. But the haphazard staging of emotional events without regard to their value as part of the whole campaign, is a waste of effort, just as it would be a waste of effort for the manufacturer of hockey skates to advertise a picture of a church surrounded by spring foliage. It is true that the church appeals to our religious impulses and that everybody loves the spring, but these impulses do not help to sell the idea that hockey skates are amusing, helpful, or increase the general enjoyment of life for the buyer.

Present-day politics places emphasis on personality. An entire party, a platform, an international policy is sold to the public, or is not sold, on the basis of the intangible element of personality. A charming candidate is the alchemist's secret that can trasmute a prosaic platform into the gold of votes. Helpful is a candidate who for some reason has caught the imagination of the country; the party and its aims are certainly more important than the personality of the candidate. Not personality, but the ability of the candidate to carry out the party's program adequately, and the program itself should be emphasized in a sound campaign plan. Even Henry Ford, the most picturesque personality in business in America today, has become known through his product, and not for his product through him.

It is essential for the campaign manager to educate the emotions in terms of groups. The public is not made up merely of Democrats and Republicans. People today are largely uninterested in politics, and their interest in the issues of the campaign must be secured by coordinating it with their personal interests. The public is made up of interlocking groups—economic, social, religious, educational, cultural, racial, collegiate, local, sports, and hundreds of others.

When President Coolidge invited actors for breakfast, he did so because he realized not only that actors were a group, but that audiences, the large group of people who like amusements, who like people who amuse them, and who like people who can be amused, ought to be aligned with him.

The Shepard-Tower Maternity Bill was passed because the people who fought to secure its passage realized that mothers made up a group, that educators made up a group, that physicians made up a group, that all these groups in turn influence other groups, and that taken all together these groups were sufficiently strong and numerous to impress Congress with the fact that the people at large wanted this bill to be made part of the national law.

The political campaign having defined its broad objects and its basic plans, having defined the group appeal which it must use, must carefully allocate to each of the media at hand the work which it can do with maximum efficiency.

The media through which a political campaign may be brought home to the public are numerous and fairly well defined. Events and activities must be created in order to put ideas into circulation, in these channels, which are as varied as the means of human communication. Every object which presents pictures or words that the public can see, everything that presents intelligible sounds, can be utilized in one way or another.

At present, the political campaigner uses for the greatest part the radio, the press, the banquet hall, the mass meeting, the lecture platform, and the stump generally as a means for furthering his ideas. But this is only a small part of what may be done. Actually there are infinitely more varied events that can be created to dramatize the campaign, and to make people talk of it. Exhibitions, contest, institutes of politics, the cooperation of education institutions, the dramatic cooperation of groups which hitherto have not been drawn into active politics, and many others may be made the vehicle for the presentation of ideas to the public.

But whatever is done must be synchronized accurately with all other forms of appeal to the public. News reaches the public through the printed word—books, magazines, letters, posters, circulars and banners, newspapers; through pictures—photographs and motion pictures; through the ear—lectures, speeches, band music, radio, campaign songs. All these must be employed by the political party if it is to succeed. One method of appeal is merely one method of appeal, and in this age wherein a thousand movements and ideas are competing for public attention, one dare not put all one's eggs into one basket.

It is understood that the methods of propaganda can be effective only with the voter who makes up his own mind on the basis of his group prejudices and desires. Where specific allegiances and loyalties exist, as in the case of boss leadership, these loyalties will operate to mollify the free will of the voter. In this close relation between the boss and his constituents lies, of course, the strength of his position in politics.

It is not necessary for the politician to be the slave of the public's group prejudices, if he can learn how to mold the mind of the voters in conformity with his own ideas of public welfare and public service. The important thing for the statesman of our age is not so much to know how to please the public, but to know how to sway the public. In theory, this education might be done by means of learned pamphlets explaining the intricacies of public questions. In actual fact, it can be done only by meeting the conditions of the public mind, by creating circumstances which set up trains of thought, by dramatizing personalities, by establishing contact with the group leaders who control the opinions of the publics.

But campaigning is only an incident in political life. The process of government is continuous. And the expert use of propaganda is more useful and fundamental, although less striking, as an aid to democratic administration, than as an aid to vote getting.

Good government can be sold to a community just as any other commodity can be sold. I often wonder whether the politicians of the future, who are responsible for maintaining the prestige and effectiveness of their party, will not endeavor to train politicians who are at the same time propagandists. I talked recently with George Olvany. He said that a certain number of Princeton men were joining Tammany Hall. If I were in his place I should have taken some of my brightest young men and set them to work for Broadway theatrical productions or apprenticed them as assistants to professional propagandists before recruiting them to the service of the party.

One reason, perhaps, why the politician today is slow to take up methods which are a commonplace in business life is that he has such ready entry to the media of communication on which his power depends.

The newspaperman looks to him for news. And by his power of giving or withholding information the politician can often effectively censor political news. But being dependent, every day of the year and for year after year, upon certain politicians for news, the newspaper reporters are obliged to work in harmony with their news sources.

The political leader must be a creator of circumstances, not only a creature of mechanical process of stereotyping and rubber stamping.

Let us suppose that he is campaigning on a low-tariff platform. He may use the modern mechanism of the radio to spread his views, but he will almost certainly use the old psychological method of approach which was old in Andrew Jackson's day, and which business has largely discarded. He will say over the radio: "Vote for me and low tariff, because the high tariff increases the cost of the things you buy." He may, it is true, have the great advantage of being able to speak by radio directly to fifty million listeners. But he is making an old-fashioned approach. He is arguing with them. He is assaulting, single-handed, the resistance of inertia.

If he were a propagandist, on the other hand, although he would still use the radio, he would use it as one instrument of a well-planned strategy. Since he is campaigning on the issue of a low tariff, he not merely would tell people that the high tariff increases the cost of the things they buy, but would create circumstances which would make his contention dramatic and self-evident. He would perhaps stage a low-tariff exhibition simultaneously in twenty cities, with exhibits illustrating the additional cost due to the tariff in force. He would see that these exhibitions were ceremoniously inaugurated by prominent men and women who were interested in a low tariff apart from any interest in his personal political fortunes. He would have groups, whose interests were especially affected by the high cost of living, institute an agitation for lower schedules. He would dramatize the issue, perhaps by having prominent men boycott woolen clothes, and go to important functions in cotton suits, until the wool schedule was reduced. He might get the opinion of social workers as to whether the high cost of wool endangers the health of the poor in winter.

In whatever ways he dramatized the issue, the attention of the public would be attracted to the question before he addressed them personally. Then, when he spoke to his millions of listeners on the radio, he would not be seeking to force an argument down the throats of a public thinking of other things and annoyed by another demand on its attention;

on the contrary, he would be answering the spontaneous questions and expressing the emotional demands of a public already keyed to a certain pitch of interest in the subject.

The importance of taking the entire world public into consideration before planning an important event is shown by the wise action of Thomas Masaryk, then Provisional President, now President of the Republic of Czechoslovakia.

Czechoslovakia officially became a free state on Monday, October 28, 1918, instead of Sunday, October 17, 1918, because Professor Masaryk realized that the people of the world would receive more information and would be more receptive to the announcement of the republic's freedom on a Monday morning than on a Sunday, because the press would have more space to devote to it on Monday morning.

Discussing the matter with me before he made the announcement, Professor Masaryk said, "I would be making history for the cables if I changed the date of Czechoslovakia's birth as a free nation." Cables make history and so the date was changed.

This incident illustrates the importance of technique in the new propaganda.

It will be objected, of course, that propaganda will tend to defeat itself as its mechanism becomes obvious to the public. My opinion is that it will not. The only propaganda which will ever tend to weaken itself as the world becomes more sophisticated and intelligent, is propaganda that is untrue or unsocial.

Again, the objection is raised that propaganda is utilized to manufacture our leading political personalities. It is asked whether, in fact, the leader makes propaganda, or whether propaganda makes the leader. There is a widespread impression that a good press agent can puff up a nobody into a great man.

The answer is the same as that made to the old query as to whether the newspaper makes public opinion or whether public opinion makes the newspaper. There has to be fertile ground for the leader and the idea to fall on. But the leader also has to have some vital seed to sow. To use another figure, a mutual need has to exist before either can become positively effective. Propaganda is of no use to the politician unless he has something to say which the public, consciously or unconsciously, wants to hear.

But even supposing that a certain propaganda is untrue or dishonest, we cannot on that account reject the methods of propaganda as such. For propaganda in some form will always be used where leaders need to appeal to their constituencies.

The criticism is often made that propaganda tends to make the President of the United States so important that he becomes not the President but the embodiment of the idea of hero worship, not to say deity worship. I quite agree that this is so, but how are you going to stop a condition which accurately reflects the desires of a certain part of the public? The American people rightly senses the enormous importance of the executive's office. If the public tends to make of the President a heroic symbol of that power, that is not the fault of propaganda but lies in the very nature of the office and its relation to the people.

This condition, despite its somewhat irrational puffing up of the man to fit the office, is perhaps still more sound than a condition in which the man utilizes no propaganda, or a propaganda not adapted to its proper end. Note the example of the Prince of Wales. This young man reaped bales of clippings and little additional glory from his American visit, merely because he was poorly advised. To the American public he became a well dressed, charming, sport-loving, dancing, perhaps frivolous youth. Nothing was done to add dignity and prestige to this impression until, towards the end of his stay, he made a trip in the subway of New York. This sole venture into democracy and the serious business of living as evidenced in the daily habits of workers, aroused new interest in the Prince. Had he been properly advised he would have augmented this somewhat by such serious studies of American life as were made by another prince, Gustave of Sweden. As a result of the lack of well directed propaganda, the Prince of Wales became in the eyes of the American people, not the thing which he constitutionally is, a symbol of the unity of the British Empire, but part and parcel of the sporting Long Island and dancing beauties of the ballroom. Great Britain lost an invaluable opportunity to increase the good will and understanding between the two countries when it failed to understand the importance of correct public relations counsel for His Royal Highness.

The public actions of America's chief executive are, if one chooses to put it that way, stage-managed. But they are chosen to represent and dramatize the man in his function as representative of the people. A political practice which has its roots in the tendency of the popular leader to follow oftener than he leads is the technique of the trial balloon which he uses in order to maintain, as he believes, his contact with the public. The politician, of course, has his ear to the ground. It might be called the clinical ear. It touches the ground and hears the disturbances of the political universe.

But he often does not know what the disturbances mean,

whether they are superficial, or fundamental. So he sends up his balloon. He may send out an anonymous interview through the press. He then waits for reverberations to come from the public—a public which expresses itself in mass meetings, or resolutions, or telegrams, or even such obvious manifestations as editorials in the partisan or nonpartisan press. On the basis of these repercussions he then publicly adopts his original tentative policy, or rejects it, or modifies it to conform to the sum of public opinion which has reached him. This method is modeled on the peace feelers which were used during the war to sound out the disposition of the enemy to make peace or to test any one of a dozen other popular tendencies. It is the method commonly used by a politician before committing himself to legislation of any kind, and by a government before committing itself on foreign or domestic policies.

It is a method which has little justification. If a politician is a real leader he will be able, by the skillful use of propaganda, to lead the people, instead of following the people by means of the clumsy instrument of trial and error.

The propagandist's approach is the exact opposite of that of the politician just described. The whole basis of successful propaganda is to have an objective and then to endeavor to arrive at it through an exact knowledge of the public and modifying circumstances to manipulate and sway that public. "The function of a statesman," says George Bernard Shaw, "is to express the will of the people in the way of a scientist."

The political leader of today should be a leader as finely versed in the technique of propaganda as in political economy and civics. If he remains merely the reflection of the average intelligence of his community, he might as well go out of politics. If one is dealing with a democracy in which the herd and the group follow those whom they recognize as leaders, why should not the young men training for leadership be trained in its technique as well as in its idealism? "When the interval between the intellectual classes and the practical classes is too great," says the historian Buckle, "the former will possess no influence, the latter will reap no benefits."

Propaganda bridges this interval in our modern complex civilization.

Only through the wise use of propaganda will our government, considered as the continuous administrative organ of the people, be able to maintain that intimate relationship with the public which is necessary in a democracy.

As David Lawrence pointed out in a recent speech, there is need for an intelligent interpretative bureau for our government in Washington. There is, it is true, a Division of Current Information in the Department of State, which at first was headed by a trained newspaperman. But later this position began to be filled by men from the diplomatic service, men who had very little knowledge of the public.

While some of these diplomats have done very well, Mr. Lawrence asserted that in the long run the country would be benefited if the functions of this office were in the hands of a different type of person.

There should, I believe, be an Assistant Secretary of State who is familiar with the problem of dispensing information to the press—some one upon whom the Secretary of State can call for consultation and who has sufficient authority to persuade the Secretary of State to make public that which, for insufficient reason, is suppressed.

The function of the propagandist is much broader

in scope than that of a mere dispenser of information to the press. The United States Government should create a Secretary of Public Relations as a member of the President's Cabinet. The function of this official should be to correctly interpret America's aims and ideals throughout the world, and to keep the citizens of this country in touch with governmental activities and the reasons which prompt them. He would, in short, interpret the people to the government and the government to the people.

Such an official would be neither a propagandist nor a press agent, in the ordinary understanding of those terms. He would be, rather, a trained technician who would be helpful in analyzing public thought and public trends in order to keep the government informed about the public, and the people informed about the government. America's relations with South America and with Europe would be greatly improved under such circumstances. Ours must be a leadership democracy administered by the intelligent minority who know how to regiment and guide the masses.

Is this government by propaganda? Call it, if you prefer, government by education. But education, in the academic sense of the word, is not sufficient. It must be enlightened expert propaganda through the creation of circumstances, through the high-spotting of significant events, and the dramatization of important issues. The statesman of the future will thus be enabled to focus the public mind on crucial points of policy and regiment a vast, heterogeneous mass of voters to clear understanding and intelligent action.

CHAPTER VII

WOMEN'S ACTIVITIES AND PROPAGANDA

Women in contemporary America have achieved a legal equality with men. This does not mean that their activities are identical with those of men. Women in the mass still have special interests and activities in addition to their economic pursuits and vocational interests.

Women's most obvious influence is exerted when they are organized and armed with the weapon of propaganda. So organized and armed they made their influence felt on city councils, state legislatures, and national congresses, upon executives, upon political campaigns and upon public opinion generally, both local and national.

In politics, the American women today occupy a much more important position, from the standpoint of their influence, in their organized groups than from the standpoint of the leadership they have required in actual political positions or in actual office holding. The professional woman politician has had, up to the present, not much influence, nor do women generally regard her as being the most important element in question. Ma Ferguson, after all, was simply a woman in the home, a catspaw for a deposed husband; Nellie

Ross, the former Governor of Wyoming, is from all accounts hardly a leader of statesmanship or public opinion.

If the suffrage campaign did nothing more, it showed the possibilities of propaganda to achieve certain ends. This propaganda today is being utilized by women to achieve their programs in Washington and in the states. In Washington they are organized as the Legislative Committee of Fourteen Women's Organizations, including the League of Women Voters, the Young Women's Christian Association, the Women's Christian Temperance Union, the Federation of Women's Clubs, etc. These organizations map out a legislative program and then use the modern technique of propaganda to make this legislative program actually pass into the law of the land. Their accomplishments in the field are various. They can justifiably take the credit for much welfare legislation. The eight-hour day is theirs. Undoubtedly prohibition and its enforcement are theirs, if they can be considered an accomplishment. So is the Shepard-Towner Bill which stipulates support by the central government of maternity welfare in the state governments. This bill would not have passed had it not been for the political prescience and sagacity of women like Mrs. Vanderlip and Mrs. Mitchell.

The Federal measures endorsed at the first convention of the National League of Women Voters typify social welfare activities of women's organizations. These covered such broad interests as child welfare, education, the home and high prices, women in gainful occupations, public health and morals, independent citizenship for married women, and others.

To propagandize these principles, the National League of Women Voters has published all types of literature, such as bulletins, calendars, election information, has held a correspondence course on government and conducted demonstration classes and citizenship schools.

Possibly the effectiveness of women's organizations in American politics today is due to two things: first, the training of a professional class of executive secretaries or legislative secretaries during the suffrage campaigns, where every device known to the propagandist had to be used to regiment a recalcitrant majority; secondly, the routing over into peacetime activities of the many prominent women who were in the suffrage campaigns and who also devoted themselves to the important drives and mass influence movements during the war. Such women as Mrs. Frank Vanderlip, Alice Ames Winter, Mrs. Henry Moskowitz, Mrs. Florence Kelley, Mrs. John Blair, Mrs. O. H. P. Belmont, Doris Stevens, Alice Paul come to mind.

If I seem to concentrate on the accomplishments of women in politics, it is because they afford a particularly striking example of the intelligent use of the new propaganda to secure attention and acceptance of minority ideas. It is perhaps curiously appropriate that the latest recruits to the political arena should recognize and make use of the newest weapons of persuasion to offset any lack of experience with what is somewhat euphemistically termed practical politics. As an example of this new technique: Some years ago, the Consumer's Committee of Women, fighting the "American valuation" tariff, rented an empty store on Fifty-Seventh Street in New York and set up an exhibit of merchandise, tagging each item with the current price and the price it would cost if the tariff went through. Hundreds of visitors to this store rallied to the cause of the committee.

But there are also nonpolitical fields in which women

can make and have made their influence felt for social ends, and in which they have utilized the principle of group leadership in attaining the desired objectives.

In the General Federation of Women's Clubs, there are 13,000 clubs. Broadly classified, they include civic and city clubs, mothers' and homemakers' clubs, cultural clubs devoted to art, music or literature, business and professional women's clubs, and general women's clubs, which may embrace either civic or community phases, or combine some of the other activities listed.

The woman's club is generally effective on behalf of health education; in furthering appreciation of the fine arts; in sponsoring legislation that affects the welfare of women and children; in playground development and park improvement; in raising standards of social or political morality; in homemaking and home economics, education and the like. In these fields, the woman's club concerns itself with efforts that are not ordinarily covered by existing agencies, and often both initiates and helps to further movements for the good of the community.

A club interested principally in homemaking and the practical arts can sponsor a cooking school for young brides and others. An example of the keen interest of women in this field of education is the cooking school recently conducted by the *New York Herald Tribune*, which held its classes in Carnegie Hall, seating almost 3,000 persons. For the several days of the cooking school, the hall was filled to capacity, rivaling the drawing power of a McCormack or a Paderewski, and refuting most dramatically the idea that women in large cities are not interested in housewifery.

A movement for the serving of milk in public schools, or

the establishment of a baby health station at the department of health will be an effort close to the heart of a club devoted to the interest of mothers and child welfare.

A music club can broaden its sphere and be of service to the community by cooperating with the local radio station in arranging better musical programs. Fighting bad music can be as militant a campaign and marshal as varied resources as any political battle.

An art club can be active in securing loan exhibitions for its city. It can also arrange traveling exhibits of the art work of its members or show the art work of schools or universities.

A literary club may step out of its charmed circle of lectures and literary lions and take a definite part in the educational life of the community. It can sponsor, for instance, a competition in the public schools for the best essay on the history of the city, or on the life of its most famous son.

Over and above the particular object for which the woman's club may have been constituted, it commonly stands ready to initiate or help any movement which has for its object a distinct public good in the community. More important, it constitutes an organized channel through which women can make themselves felt as a definite part of public opinion.

Just as women supplement men in private life, so they will supplement men in public life by concentrating their organized efforts on those objects which men are likely to ignore. There is a tremendous field for women as active protagonists of new ideas and new methods of political and social housekeeping. When organized and conscious of their power to influence their surroundings, women can use their newly acquired freedom in a great many ways to mold the world into a better place to live.

CHAPTER VIII

PROPAGANDA FOR EDUCATION

Education is not securing its proper share of public interest. The public school system, materially and financially, is being adequately supported. There is marked eagerness for a college education, and a vague aspiration for culture, expressed in innumerable courses and lectures. The public is not cognizant of the real value of education, and does not realize that education as a social force is not receiving the kind of attention it has the right to expect in a democracy.

It is felt, for example, that education is entitled to more space in the newspapers; that well informed discussion of education hardly exists; that unless such an issue as the Gary school system is created, or outside of an occasional discussion, such as that aroused over Harvard's decision to establish a school of business, education does not attract the active interest of the public.

There are a number of reasons for this condition. First of all, there is the fact that the educator has been trained to stimulate to thought the individual students in his classroom, but has not been trained as an educator at large of the public.

In a democracy an educator should, in addition to his

academic duties, bear a definite and wholesome relation to the general public. This public does not come within the immediate scope of his academic duties. But in a sense he depends upon it for his living, for the moral support, and the general cultural tone upon which his work must be based. In the field of education, we find what we have found in politics and other fields—that the evolution of the practioner of the profession has not kept pace with the social evolution around him, and is out of gear with the instruments for the dissemination of ideas which modern society has developed. If this be true, then the training of the educators in this respect should begin in the normal schools, with the addition to their curricula of wherever is necessary to broaden their viewpoint. The public cannot understand unless the teacher understands the relationship between the general public and the academic idea. The normal school should provide for the training of the educator to make him realize that his is a twofold job: education as a teacher and education as a propagandist.

A second reason for the present remoteness of education from the thoughts and interests of the public is found in the mental attitude of the pedagogue—whether primary school teacher or college professor—toward the world outside the school. This is a difficult psychological problem. The teacher finds himself in a world in which the emphasis is put on those objective goals and those objective attainments which are prized by our American society. He himself is but moderately or poorly paid. Judging himself by the standards in common acceptance, he cannot but feel a sense of inferiority because he finds himself continually being compared, in the minds of his own pupils, with the successful businessman and the successful leader in the outside world. Thus the educator becomes repressed and suppressed in our civilization. As things stand, this condition cannot be changed from the outside unless the general public alters its standards of achievement, which it is not likely to do soon.

Yet it can be changed by the teaching profession itself, if it becomes conscious not only of its individualistic relation to pupil, but also of its social relation to the general public. The teaching profession, as such, has the right to carry on a very definite propaganda with a view to enlightening the public asserting its intimate relation to the society which it serves. In addition to conducting a propaganda on behalf of its individual members, education must also raise the general appreciation of the teaching profession. Unless the profession can raise itself by its own bootstraps, it will fast lose the power of recruiting outstanding talent for itself.

Propaganda cannot change all that is at present unsatisfactory in the educational situation. There are factors, such as low pay and the lack of adequate provision for superannuated teachers, which definitely affect the status of the profession. It is possible, by means of an intelligent appeal predicated upon the actual present composition of the public mind, to modify the general attitude toward the teaching profession. Such a changed attitude will begin by expressing itself in an insistence on the idea of more adequate salaries for the profession.

There are various ways in which academic organizations in America handle their financial problems. One type of college or university depends for its monetary support upon grants from the state legislatures. Another depends upon private endowment. There are other types of education institutes, such as sectarian, but the two chief types include by far the greater number of our institutions of higher learning.

The state university is supported by grants from the people of the state, voted by the state legislature. In theory, the degree of support which the university receives is dependent upon the degree of acceptance accorded it by the voters. The state university prospers according to the extent to which it can sell itself to the people of the state.

The state university is therefore in an unfortunate position unless its president happens to be a man of outstanding merit as a propagandist and a dramatizer of educational issues. Yet if this is the case—if the university shapes its whole policy toward gaining the support of the state legislature—its educational function may suffer. It may be tempted to base its whole appeal to the public on its public service, real or supposed, and permit the education of its individual students to take care of itself. It may attempt to educate the people of the state at the expense of its own pupils. This may generate a number of evils, to the extent of making the university a political instrument, a mere tool of the political group in power. If the president dominates both the public and the professional politician, this may lead to a situation in which the personality of the president outweighs the true function of the institution.

The endowed college or university has a problem quite as perplexing. The endowed college is dependent upon the support, usually, of key men in industry whose social and economic objectives are concrete and limited, and therefore often at variance with the pursuit of abstract knowledge.

The successful businessman criticizes the great universities for being too academic, but seldom for being too practical. One might imagine that the key men who support our universities would like them to specialize in schools of applied science, of practical salesmanship, or of industrial efficiency. And it may well be, in many instances, that the demands which the potential endowers of our universities make upon these institutions are flatly in contradiction to the interests of scholarship and general culture.

We have, therefore, the anomalous situation of the college seeking to carry on a propaganda in favor of scholarship among people who are quite out of sympathy with the aims to which they are asked to subscribe their money. Men who, by the commonly accepted standards, are failures or very moderate successes in our American World (the pedagogues) seek to convince the outstanding successes (the businessmen) that they should give their money to ideals which they do not pursue. Men who, through a sense of inferiority, despise money, seek to win the good will of men who love money.

It seems possible that the future status of the endowed college will depend upon a balancing of these forces, with both the academic and the endowed elements obtaining in effect due consideration.

The college must win public support. If the potential donor is apathetic, enthusiastic public approval must be obtained to convince him. If he seeks unduly to influence the educational policy of the institution, public opinion must support the college in the continuance of its proper functions. If either factor dominates unduly, we are likely to find a demagoguery or a snobbishness aiming to please one group or the other.

There is still another potential solution of the problem.

It is possible, through an education propaganda aiming to develop greater social consciousness on the part of the people of the country, that there may be awakened in the minds of men of affairs, as a class, social consciousness which will produce more minds of the type of Julius Rosenwald, V. Everitt Macy, John D. Rockefeller Jr., the late Willard Straight.

Many colleges have already developed intelligent propaganda in order to bring them into active and continuous relation with the general public. A definite technique has been developed in their relation to the community in the form of college news bureaus. These bureaus have formed an intercollegiate association whose members meet once a year to discuss their problems. These problems include the education of the alumnus and his effect upon the general public and upon specific groups, the education of the future student to the choice of the particular college, the maintenance of an *esprit de corps* so that the athletic prowess of the college will not be placed first, the development of some familiarity with the research work done in the college in order to attract the attention of those who may be able to lend aid, the development of an understanding of the aims and the work of the institution in order to attract special endowments for specified purposes.

Some seventy-five of these bureaus are now affiliated with the American Association of College News Bureaus, including those of Yale, Wellesley, Illinois, Indiana, Wisconsin, Western Reserve, Tufts, and California. A bimonthly news letter is published, bringing to members the news of their profession. The Association endeavors to uphold the ethical standards of the profession and aims to work in harmony with the press.

The National Education Association and other societies are carrying on a definite propaganda to promote the larger purposes of education endeavor. One of the aims of such propaganda is of course improvement in the prestige and material position of the teachers themselves. An occasional McAndrew case calls the attention of the public to the fact that in some schools the teacher is far from enjoying full academic freedom, while in certain communities the choice of teachers is based upon political or sectarian considerations rather than upon real ability. If such issues were made, by means of propaganda, to become a matter of public concern on a truly national scale, there would doubtless be a general tendency to improvement.

The concrete problems of colleges are more varied and puzzling than one might suppose. The pharmaceutical college of a university is concerned because the drug store is no longer merely a drug store, but primarily a soda fountain, a lunch counter, a bookshop, a retailer of all sorts of general merchandise from society stationery to spare radio parts. The college realizes the economic utility of the lunch counter feature to the practicing druggist, yet it feels that the ancient and honorable art of compounding specifics is being degraded.

Cornell University discovers that endowments are rare. Why? Because the people think that the University is a state institution and therefore publicly supported.

Many of our leading universities rightly feel that the results of their scholarly researches should not only be presented to libraries and learned publications, but should also, where practicable and useful, be given to the public in the dramatic form which the public can understand. Harvard is but one example.

"Not long ago," says Charles A. Merrill in *Personality*, "a certain Harvard professor vaulted into the newspaper headlines. There were several days when one could hardly pick up a paper in any of the larger cities without finding his name bracketed with his achievement.

"The professor, who was back from a trip to Yucatan in the interests of science, had solved the mystery of the Venus calendar of the ancient Mayas. He had discovered the key to the puzzle of how the Mayas kept tab on the flight of time. Checking the Mayan record of celestial events against the known astronomical facts, he had found a perfect correlation between the time count of these Central American Indians and the true positions of the planet Venus in the sixth century B.C. A civilization which flourished in the Western Hemisphere twenty-five centuries ago was demonstrated to have attained heights hitherto unappreciated by the modern world.

"How the professor's discovery happened to be chronicled in the popular press is, also, in retrospect, a matter of interest.... If left to his own devices, he might never have appeared in print, except perhaps in some technical publication, and his remarks there would have been no more intelligible to the average man or woman than if they had been inscribed in Mayan hieroglyphics.

"Popularization of this message from antiquity was due to the initiative of a young man named James W. D. Seymour...

"It might surprise and shock some people," Mr. Merrill

adds, "to be told that the oldest and most dignified seats of learning in America now hire press agents, just as railroad companies, fraternal organizations, moving picture producers and political parties retain them. It is nevertheless a fact....

"...there is hardly a college or university in the country which does not, with the approval of the governing body and the faculty, maintain a publicity office, with a director and a staff of assistants, for the purpose of establishing friendly relations with the newspapers, and through the newspapers, with the public..."

"This enterprise breaks sharply with tradition. In the older seats of learning it is a recent innovation. It violates the fundamental article in the creed of the old academic societies. Cloistered seclusion used to be considered the first essential of scholarship. The college was anxious to preserve its aloofness from the world....

"The colleges used to resent outside interest in their affairs. They might, somewhat reluctantly and contemptuously, admit reporters to their Commencement Day exercise, but no further would they go...

'Today, if a newspaper reporter wants to interview a Harvard professor, he has merely to telephone the Secretary for Information to the University. Officially, Harvard still shies away from the title 'Director of Publicity.' Informally, however, the secretary with the long title is the publicity man. He is an important official today at Harvard."

It may be a new idea that the president of a university will concern himself with the kind of mental picture his institution produces on the public mind. Yet it is part of the president's work to see that his university takes its proper place in the community and therefore also in the community mind, and produces the results desired, both in a cultural and in a financial sense.

If his institution does not produce the mental picture which it should, one of two things may be wrong: Either the media of communication with the public may be wrong or unbalanced; or his institution may be at fault. The public is getting an oblique impression of the university, in which case the impression should be modified; or it may be that the public is getting a correct impression, in which case, very possibly, the work of the university itself should be modified. For both possibilities lie within the province of the public relations counsel.

Columbia University recently instituted a *Casa Italiana*, which was solemnly inaugurated in the presence of representatives of the Italian government, to emphasize its high standing in Latin Studies and the Romance languages. Years ago Harvard founded the Germanic Museum, which was ceremoniously opened by Prince Henry of Prussia.

Many colleges maintain extension courses which bring their work to the knowledge of a broad public. It is of course proper that such courses should be made known to the general public. But, to take another example, if they have been badly planned, from the point of view of public relations, if they are unduly scholastic and detached, their effect may be the opposite of favorable. In such a case, it is not the work of the public relations counsel to urge that the courses be made better known, but to urge that they first be modified to conform to the impression which the college wishes to create, where that is compatible with the university's scholastic ideas.

Again, it may be the general opinion that the work of

a certain institution is 80 percent postgraduate research, an opinion which may tend to alienate public interest. This opinion may be true or it may be false. If it is false, it should be corrected by high-spotting undergraduate activities.

If, on the other hand, it is true that 80 percent of the work is postgraduate research, the most should be made of that fact. It should be the concern of the president to make known the discoveries which are of possible public interest. A university expedition in Biblical lands may be uninteresting as a purely scholastic undertaking, but if it contributes light on some Biblical assertion it will immediately arouse the interest of large masses of the population. The zoological department may be hunting for some strange bacillus which has no known relation to any human disease, but the fact that it is chasing bacilli is in itself capable of dramatic presentation to the public.

Many universities now gladly lend members of their faculties to assist in investigations of public interest. Thus Cornell lent Professor Wilcox to aid the government in the preparation of the national census. Professor Irving Fisher of Yale has been called in to advise on currency matters.

In the ethical sense, propaganda bears the same relation to education as to business or politics. It may be abused. It may be used to over-advertise an institution and to create in the public mind artificial values. There can be no absolute guarantee against its misuse.

CHAPTER IX

PROPAGANDA IN SOCIAL SERVICE

The public relations counsel is necessary to social work. And since social service, by its very nature, can continue only by means of the voluntary support of the wealthy, it is obliged to use propaganda continually. The leaders in social service were among the first to consciously utilize propaganda in its modern sense.

The great enemy of any attempt to change men's habits is inertia. Civilization is limited by inertia.

Our attitude toward social relations, toward economics, toward national and international politics, continues past attitudes and strengthens them under the force of tradition. Comstock drops his mantle of proselytizing morality on the willing shoulders of a Sumner; Penrose drops his mantle on Butler; Carnegie his on Schwab, and so *ad infinitum*. Opposing this traditional acceptance of existing ideas is an active public opinion that has been directed consciously into movements against inertia. Public opinion was made or changed formerly by tribal chiefs, by kings, by religious leaders. Today the privilege of attempting to sway public opinion is everyone's. It is one of the manifestations of democracy that any one may try to convince others and to assume leadership on behalf of his own thesis.

New ideas, new precedents, are continually striving for a place in the scheme of things.

The social settlement, the organized campaigns against tuberculosis and cancer, the various research activities aiming directly at the elimination of social diseases and maladjustments—a multitude of altruistic activities which could be catalogued only in a book of many pages—have need of knowledge of the public mind and mass psychology if they are to achieve their aims. The literature on social service publicity is so extensive, and the underlying principles so fundamental, that only one example is necessary here to illustrate the technique of social service propaganda.

A social service organization undertook to fight lynching, Jim Crowism and the civil discriminations against the Negro below the Mason and Dixon line.

The National Association for the Advancement of Colored People had the fight in hand. As a matter of technique they decided to dramatize the year's campaign in an annual convention which would concentrate attention on the problem.

Should it be held in the North, South, West, or East? Since the purpose was to affect the entire country, the association was advised to hold it in the South. For, said the propagandist, a point of view on southern questions, emanating from a southern center, would have greater authority than the same point of view issuing from any other locality, particularly when that point of view was at odds with the traditional southern point of view. Atlanta was chosen.

The third step was to surround the conference with people who were stereotypes for ideas that carried weight all over the country. The support of leaders of diversified groups was sought. Telegrams and letters were dispatched to leaders of religious, political, social and educational groups, asking for their point of view on the purpose of the conference. But in addition to these group leaders of national standing it was particularly important from the technical standpoint to secure the opinions of group leaders of the South, even from Atlanta itself, to emphasize the purposes of the conference to the entire public. There was one group in Atlanta which could be approached. A group of ministers had been bold enough to come out for a greater interracial amity. This group was approached and agreed to cooperate in the conference.

The event ran off as scheduled. The program itself followed the general scheme. Negroes and white men from the South, on the same platform, expressed the same point of view.

A dramatic element was spotlighted here and there. A national leader from Massachusetts agreed in principle and in practice with a Baptist preacher from the South.

If the radio had been in effect, the whole country might have heard and been moved by the speeches and the principles expressed.

But the public read the words and the ideas in the press of the country. For the event had been created of such important component parts as to awaken interest throughout the country and to gain support for its ideas even in the South.

The editorials in the southern press, reflecting the public opinion of their communities, showed that the subject had become one of interest to the editors because of the participation by southern leaders.

The event naturally gave the Association itself substantial weapons with which to appeal to an increasingly wider circle. Further publicity was attained by mailing reports, letters, and other propaganda to selected groups of the public.

As for the practical results, the immediate one was a change in the minds of many southern editors who realized that the question at issue was not only an emotional one, but also a discussable one; and this point of view was immediately reflected to their readers. Further results are hard to measure with a slide-rule. The conference had its definite effect in building up the racial consciousness and solidarity of the Negroes. The decline in lynching is very probably a result of this and other efforts of the Association.

Many churches have made paid advertising and organized propaganda part of their regular activities. They have developed church advertising committees, which make use of the newspaper and the billboard, as well as of the pamphlet. Many denominations maintain their own periodicals. The Methodist Board of publication and Information systematically gives announcements and releases to the press and the magazines.

But in a broader sense the very activities of social service are propaganda activities. A campaign for the preservation of the teeth seeks to alter people's habits in the direction of more frequent bushing of teeth. A campaign for better parks seeks to alter people's opinion in regard to the desirability of taxing themselves for the purchase of park facilities. A Campaign against tuberculosis is an attempt to convince everybody that tuberculosis can be cured, that persons with certain symptoms should immediately go to the doctor, and the like. A campaign to lower the infant mortality rate is an effort to alter the habits of mothers in regard to feeding, bathing, and caring for their babies. Social service, in fact, is identical with propaganda in many cases.

Even those aspects of social service which are governmental and administrative, rather than charitable and spontaneous, depend on wise propaganda for their effectiveness. Professor Harry Elmer Barnes, in his book, *The Evolution of Modern Penology in Pennsylvania*, states that improvements in penological administration in the state are hampered by political influences. The legislature must be persuaded to permit the utilization of the best methods of scientific penology, and for this there is necessary the development of an enlightened public opinion. "Until such a situation has been brought about," Mr. Barnes states, "progress in penology is doomed to be sporadic, local, and generally ineffective. The solution of prison problems, then, seems to be fundamentally a problem of conscientious and scientific publicity."

Social progress is simply the progressive education and enlightenment of the public mind in regard to its immediate and distant social problems.

CHAPTER X

ART AND SCIENCE

In the education of the American public toward greater art appreciation, propaganda plays an important part. When art galleries seek to launch the canvases of an artist they should create public acceptance for his works. To increase public appreciation a deliberate propagandizing effort must be made.

In art as in politics the minority rules, but it can rule only by going out to meet the public on its own ground, by understanding the anatomy of public opinion and utilizing it.

In applied and commercial art, propaganda makes greater opportunities for the artist than ever before. This arises from the fact that mass production reaches an impasse when it competes on a price basis only. It must, therefore, in a large number of fields create a field of competition bases on aesthetic values. Business of many types capitalizes the aesthetic values. Business of many types capitalizes the aesthetic sense to increase markets and profits. Which is only another way of saying that the artist has the opportunity of collaborating with industry in such a way as to improve the public taste, injecting beautiful instead of ugly motifs in the articles of common use, and, furthermore, securing recognition and money for himself.

Propaganda can play a part in pointing out what is and what is not beautiful, and business can definitely help in this way to raise the level of American culture. In this process propaganda will naturally make use of the authority of group leaders whose taste and opinion are recognized.

The public must be interested by means of associational values and dramatic incidents. New inspiration, which to the artist may be a very technical and abstract kind of beauty, must be made vital to the public by association with values which it recognizes and responds to.

For instance, in the manufacture of American silk, markets are developed by going to Paris for inspiration. Paris can give American silk a stamp of authority which will aid it to achieve definite position in the United States.

The following clipping from the *New York Times* of February 16, 1925, tells the story from an actual incident of this sort:

"Copyright, 1925, by *THE NEW YORK TIMES* COMPANY—Special Cable to *THE NEW YORK TIMES.*

"PARIS, Feb. 15—For the first time in history, American art materials are to be exhibited in the Decorative Arts Section of the Louvre Museum.

"The exposition opening on May 26th with the Minister of Fine Arts, Paul Leon, acting as patron, will include silk from Cheney Brothers, South Manchester and New York, the designs of which were based on the inspiration of Edgar

Brands, famous French iron worker, the modern Bellini, who makes wonderful art works from iron.

"M. Brandt designed and made the monumental iron doors of the Verdun war memorial. He has been asked to assist and participate in this exposition, which will show France the accomplishments of American industrial art.

"Thirty designs inspired by Edgar Brandt's work are embodied in 2,500 yards of printed silks, tinsels and cut velvets in a hundred colors…

"These 'prints ferronnières' are the first textiles to show the influence of the modern master, M. Brandt. The silken fabrics possess a striking composition, showing characteristic Brandt motifs which were embodied in the tracery of large designs by the Cheney artists who succeeded in translating the iron into silk, a task which might appear almost impossible. The strength and brilliancy of the original design is enhanced by the beauty and warmth of color."

The result of this ceremony was that prominent department stores in New York, Chicago, and other cities asked to have this exhibition. They tried to mold the public taste in conformity with the idea which had the approval of Paris. The silks of Cheney Brothers—a commercial product produced in quantity—gained a place in public esteem by being associated with the work of a recognized artist and with a great art museum.

The same can be said of almost any commercial product susceptible of beautiful design. There are few products in daily use, whether furniture, clothes, lamps, posters, commercial labels, book jackets, pocketbooks or bathtubs which are not subject to the laws of good taste.

In America, whole departments of production are being changed through propaganda to fill an economic as well as an aesthetic need. Manufacture is being modified to conform to the economic need to satisfy the public demand for more beauty. A piano manufacturer recently engaged artists to design modernist pianos. This was not done because there existed a widespread demand for modernist pianos. Indeed, the manufacturer probably expected to sell few. But in order to draw attention to pianos one must have something more than a piano. People at tea parties will not talk about pianos; but they may talk about the new modernist piano.

When Secretary Hoover, three years ago, was asked to appoint a commission to the Paris Exposition of Decorative Arts, he did so. As Associate Commissioner I assisted in the organizing of the group of important business leaders in the industrial art field who went to Paris as delegates to visit and report on the Exposition. The propaganda carried on for the aims and purposes of the Commission undoubtedly had a widespread effect on the attitude of Americans towards art in industry: it was only a few years later that the modern art movement penetrated all fields of industry.

Department stores took it up. R.H. Macy & Company held an Art-in-Trades Exposition, in which the Metropolitan Museum of Art collaborated as adviser. Lord & Taylor sponsored a Modern Arts Exposition, with foreign exhibitors. These stores, coming closely in touch with the life of the people, performed a propagandizing function in bringing to the people the best in art as it related to these industries. The Museum at the same time was alive to the importance of making contact with the public mind, by utilizing the department store to increase art appreciation.

Of all art institutions the museum suffers most from the lack of effective propaganda. Most present-day museums have the reputation of being morgues or sanctuaries, whereas they should be leaders and teachers in the aesthetic life of the community. They have little vital relation to life.

The treasures of beauty in a museum need to be interpreted to the public, and this requires a propagandist. The housewife in a Bronx apartment doubtless feels little interest in an ancient Greek vase in the Metropolitan Museum. Yet an artist working with a pottery firm may adapt the design of this vase to a set of china and this china, priced low through quantity production, may find its way to that Bronx apartment, developing unconsciously, through its fine line and color, an appreciation of beauty.

Some American museums feel this responsibility. The Metropolitan Museum of Art of New York rightly prides itself on its million and a quarter of visitors in the year 1926; on its efforts to dramatize and make visual the civilizations which its various departments reveal; on its special lectures, its story hours, its loan collections of prints and photographs and lantern slides, its facilities offered to commercial firms in the field of applied art, on the outside lecturers who are invited to lecture in its auditorium and on the lectures given by its staff to outside organizations; and on the free chamber concerts given in the museum under the direction of David Mannes, which tend to dramatize the museum as home of beauty. Yet that is not the whole of the problem.

It is not merely a question of making people come to the museum. It is also a question of making the museum, and the beauty which it houses, go to the people.

The museum's accomplishments should not be evaluated

merely in terms of the number of visitors. Its function is not merely to receive visitors, but to project itself and what it stands for in the community which it serves.

The museum can stand in its community for a definite aesthetic standard which can, by the help of intelligent propaganda, permeate the daily lives of all its neighbors. Why should not a museum establish a museum council of art, to establish standards in home decoration, in architecture, and in commercial production? Or a research board for applied arts? Why should not the museum, instead of merely preserving the art treasures which it possesses, quicken their meaning in terms which the general public understands?

A recent annual report of an art museum in one of the large cities of the United States says: "An underlying characteristic of an art Museum like ours must be its attitude of conservatism, for after all its first duty is to treasure the great achievements of men in the arts and sciences."

Is that true? Is not another important duty to interpret the models of beauty which it possesses?

If the duty of the museum is to be active it must study how best to make its message intelligible to the community which it serves. It must bodily assume aesthetic leadership.

As in art, so in science, both pure and applied. Pure science was once guarded and fostered by learned societies and scientific associations. Now pure science finds support and encouragement also in industry. Many of the laboratories in which abstract research is being pursued are now connected with some large corporation, which is quite willing to devote hundreds of thousands of dollars to scientific study, for the sake of one golden invention or discovery which may emerge from it.

Big business of course gains heavily when the invention emerges. But at that very moment it assumes the responsibility of placing the new invention at the service of the public. It assumes also the responsibility of interpreting its meaning to the public.

The industrial interests can furnish to the schools, the colleges, and the postgraduate university courses the exact truth concerning the scientific progress of our age. They not only can do so; they are under obligation to do so. Propaganda as an instrument of commercial competition has opened opportunities to the inventor and given great stimulus to the research scientist. In the last five or ten years, the successes of some of the larger corporations have been so outstanding that the whole field of science has received a tremendous impetus. The American Telephone and Telegraph Company, the Western Electric Company, the General Electric Company, the Westinghouse Electric Company and others have realized the importance of scientific research. They have also understood that their ideas must be made intelligible to the public to be fully successful. Television, broadcasting, loud speakers are utilized as propaganda aids.

Propaganda assists in marketing new inventions. Propaganda, by repeatedly interpreting new scientific ideas and inventions to the public, has made the public more receptive. Propaganda is accustoming the public to change and progress.

CHAPTER XI

THE MECHANICS OF PROPAGANDA

The media by which special pleaders transmit their messages to the public through propaganda include all the means by which people today transmit their ideas to one another. There is no means of human communication which may not also be a means of deliberate propaganda, because propaganda is simply the establishing of reciprocal understanding between an individual and a group.

The important point to the propagandist is that the relative value of the various instruments of propaganda, and their relation to the masses, are constantly changing. If he is to get full reach for his message he must take advantage of these shifts of value the instant they occur. Fifty years ago, the public meeting was a propaganda instrument par excellence. Today it is difficult to get more than a handful of people to attend a public meeting unless extraordinary attractions are part of the program. The automobile takes them away from home, the radio keeps them in the home, the successive daily editions of the newspaper bring information to them in office or subway, and they are also sick of the ballyhoo of the rally.

Instead there are numerous other media of communication, some new, others old but so transformed that they have become virtually new. The newspaper, of course, remains always a primary medium for the transmission of opinions and ideas—in other words, for propaganda.

It was not many years ago that newspaper editors resented what they called "the use of the news columns for propaganda purposes." Some editors would even kill a good story if they imagined its publication might benefit anyone. This point of view is not largely abandoned. Today the leading editorial offices take the view that the real criterion governing the publication or nonpublication of matter which comes to the desk is its news value. The newspaper cannot assume, nor is it its function to assume, the responsibility of guaranteeing that what it publishes will not work out to somebody's interest. There is hardly a single item in any daily paper, the publication of which does not, or might not, profit or injure somebody. That is the nature of news. What the newspaper does strive for is that the news which it publishes shall be accurate, and (since it must select from the mass of news material available) that it shall be of interest and importance to large groups of its readers.

In its editorial columns the newspaper is a personality, commenting upon things and events from its individual point of view. But in its news columns the typical modern American newspaper attempts to reproduce, with due regard to news interest, the outstanding events and opinions of the day.

It does not ask whether a given item is propaganda or not. What is important is that it be news. And in the selection of news the editor is usually entirely independent. In the

New York Times—to take an outstanding example—news is printed because of its news value and for no other reason. The *Times'* editors determine with complete independence what is and what is not news. They brook no censorship. They are not influenced by any external pressure nor swayed by any values of expediency or opportunism. The conscientious editor on every newspaper realizes that his obligation to the public is news. The fact of its accomplishments makes it news.

If the public relations counsel can breathe the breath of life into an idea and make it take its place among other ideas and events, it will receive the public attention it merits. There can be no question of his "contaminating news at its source." He creates some of the day's events, which must compete in the editorial office with other events. Often the events which he creates may be specially acceptable to a newspaper's public and he may create them with that public in mind.

If important things of life today consist of transatlantic radiophone talks arranged by commercial telephone companies; if they consist of inventions that will be commercially advantageous to the men who market them; if they consist of Henry Fords with epoch-making cars—then all this is news. The so-called flow of propaganda into the newspaper offices of the country may, simply at the editor's discretion, find its way to the wastebasket.

The source of the news offered to the editor should always be clearly stated and the facts accurately presented.

The situation of the magazines at the present moment, from the propagandist's point of view, is different from that of the daily newspapers. The average magazine assumes no obligation, as the newspaper does, to reflect the current news. It selects its material deliberately, in accordance with a continuous policy. It is not, like the newspaper, an organ of public opinion, but tends rather to become a propagandist organ, propagandizing for a particular idea, whether it be good housekeeping, or smart apparel, or beauty in home decoration, or debunking public opinion, or general enlightenment or liberalism or amusement. One magazine may aim to sell health; another, English gardens; another, fashionable men's wear; another, Nietzschean philosophy.

In all departments in which the various magazines specialize, the public relations counsel may play an important part. For he may, because of his client's interest, assist them to create the events which further their propaganda. A bank, in order to emphasize the importance of its women's department, may arrange to supply a leading women's magazine with a series of articles and advice on investments written by the woman expert in charge of this department. The women's magazine in turn will utilize this new feature as a means of building additional prestige and circulation.

The lecture, once a powerful means of influencing public opinion, has changed its value. The lecture itself may only be a symbol, a ceremony; its importance, for propaganda purposes, lies in the fact that it was delivered. Professor So-and-So, expounding an epoch-making invention, may speak to five hundred persons, or only fifty. His lecture, if it is important, will be broadcast; report of it will appear in the newspapers; discussion will be stimulated. The real value of the lecture, from the propaganda point of view, is in its repercussion to the general public.

The radio is at present one of the most important tools

of the propagandist. Its future development is uncertain.

It may compete with the newspaper as an advertising medium. Its ability to reach millions of persons simultaneously naturally appeals to the advertiser. And since the average advertiser has a limited appropriation for advertising, money spent on the radio will tend to be withdrawn from the newspaper.

To what extent is the publisher alive to this new phenomenon? It is bound to come close to American journalism and publishing. Newspapers have recognized the advertising potentialities of the companies that manufacture radio apparatus, and of radio stores, large and small; and newspapers have accorded to the radio in their news and feature columns an importance relative to the increasing attention given by the public to radio. At the same time, certain newspapers have brought radio stations and linked them up with the news and entertainment distribution facilities, supplying these two features over the air to the public.

It is possible that newspaper chains will sell schedules of advertising space on the air and on the paper. Newspaper chains will possibly contract with advertisers for circulation on paper and over the air. There are, at present, publishers who sell space in the air and in their columns, but they regard the two as separate ventures.

Large groups, political, racial, sectarian, economic or professional, are tending to control stations to propagandize their points of view. Or is it conceivable that America may adopt the English licensing system under which the listener, instead of the advertiser, pays?

Whether the present system is changed, the

advertiser—and propagandist—must necessarily adapt himself to it. Whether, in the future, air space will be sold openly as such, or whether the message will reach the public in the form of straight entertainment and news, or as special programs for particular groups, the propagandist must be prepared to meet the conditions and utilize them.

The American motion picture is the greatest unconscious carrier of propaganda in the world today. It is a great distributor for ideas and opinions.

The motion picture can standardize the ideas and habits of a nation. Because pictures are made to meet market demands, they reflect, emphasize and even exaggerate broad popular tendencies, rather than stimulate new ideas and opinions. The motion picture avails itself only of ideas and facts which are in vogue. As the newspaper seeks to purvey news, it seeks to purvey entertainment.

Another instrument of propaganda is the personality. Has the device of the exploited personality been pushed too far? President Coolidge photographed on his vacation in full Indian regalia in company with full-blooded chiefs, was the climax of a greatly over-reported vacation. Obviously a public personality can be made absurd by misuse of the very mechanism which helped create it.

Yet the vivid dramatization of personality will always remain one of the functions of the public relations counsel. The public instinctively demands a personality to typify a conspicuous corporation or enterprise.

There is a story that a great financier discharged a partner because he had divorced his wife.

"But what," asked the partner, "have my private affairs to do with the banking business?"

"If you are not capable of managing your own wife," was the reply, "the people will certainly believe that you are not capable of managing their money."

The propagandist must treat personality as he would treat any other objective fact within his province.

A personality may create circumstances, as Lindbergh created good will between the United States and Mexico. Events may create a personality, as the Cuban War created the political figure of Roosevelt. It is often difficult to say which creates the other. Once a public figure has decided what ends he wishes to achieve, he must regard himself objectively and present an outward picture of himself which is consistent with his real character and his aims.

There are a multitude of other avenues of approach to the public mind, some old, some new as television. No attempt will be made to discuss each one separately. The school may disseminate information concerning scientific facts. The fact that a commercial concern may eventually profit from a widespread understanding of its activities because of this does not condemn the dissemination of such information, provided that the subject merits study on the part of the students. If a baking corporation contributed pictures and charts to a school to show how bread is made, these propaganda activities, if they are accurate and candid, are in no way reprehensible, provided the school authorities accept or reject such offers carefully on their educational merits.

It may be that a new product will be announced to the public by means of a motion picture or a parade taking place a thousand miles away. Or the manufacturer of a new jitney airplane may personally appear and speak in a million homes through radio and television. The man who would most effectively transmit his message to the public must be alert to make use of all the means of propaganda. Undoubtedly the public is becoming aware of the methods which are being used to mold its opinions and habits. If the public is better informed about the processes of its life, it will be so much the more receptive to reasonable appeals to its own interests. No matter how sophisticated, how cynical the public may become about publicity methods, it must respond to the basic appeals, because it will always need food, crave amusement, long for beauty, respond to leadership.

If the public becomes more intelligent in its commercial demands, commercial firms will meet the new standards. If it becomes weary of the old methods used to persuade it to accept a given idea or commodity, its leaders will present their appeals more intelligently.

Propaganda will never die out. Intelligent men must realize that propaganda is the modern instrument by which they can fight for productive ends and help to bring order out of chaos.

Printed in the United States of America

Ig Publishing
Box 2547
New York, NY 10163
www.igpub.com

Library of Congress Cataloging-in-Publication Data

Bernays, Edward L., 1891-1995
Propaganda/Edward Bernays; introduction by Mark Crispin Miller. p. cm.
Originally published: New York: H. Liveright, 1928.
ISBN-10: 0-9703125-9-8 ISBN-13: 978-0-9703125-9-4
1. Propaganda. 1. Title.
HM1231.B47 2005
303.3'75-dc22

2004016015

PROPAGANDA

EDWARD BERNAYS

With an Introduction by Mark Crispin Miller

New York, NY